Even when faced with overwhelming affliction, it is possible to

TAKE HEART!

The lives of Bruce and Lory Lockerbie and their family were instantaneously changed when Bruce suffered a heart attack at the age of 46. In this personal narrative, the Lockerbies reveal their responses to Bruce's close brush with death. They share how feelings of helplessness, anger, frustration, and fear eventually gave way to a deeper, stronger faith in God.

Certainly no couple wants to consider that their family may be afflicted by a critical illness. Yet over one million people suffer from heart attacks in the United States each year. The Lockerbies' lessons in coping with a life-threatening crisis will show others how to trust God when adversity strikes.

"So we pray for grace, in all the afflictions of life, to take heart by believing God's promises and living by them, in sure and certain hope of the resurrection to eternal life."

Bruce & Lory Lockerbie

Fleming H. Revell
Old Tappan, New Jersey

Unless otherwise identified, all Scripture quotations in this book are taken from the King James Version of the Bible.

Scripture quotations identified RSV are from the Revised Standard Version of the Bible, Copyrighted © 1946, 1952, 1971 by the Division of Christian Education of the National Council of the Churches of Christ in the United States of America, and are used by permission. All rights reserved.

Library of Congress Cataloging-in-Publication Data

Lockerbie, Bruce.
    Take heart / Bruce and Lory Lockerbie.
      p. cm.
    ISBN 0-8007-1639-6
    1. Death—Religious aspects—Christianity. 2. Lockerbie, Bruce. 3. Lockerbie, Lory. I. Lockerbie, Lory. II. Title.
BT825.L6147   1990
242'.4—dc20   89-48632
                                                         CIP

Copyright © 1990 by Bruce and Lory Lockerbie
Published by the Fleming H. Revell Company
Old Tappan, New Jersey 07675
Printed in the United States of America

To our grandchildren

. . . But immediately he spoke to them and said, "Take heart, it is I; have no fear." And he got into the boat with them and the wind ceased. . . .

Mark 6:50, 51 RSV

I fear no foe, with thee at hand to bless;
Ills have no weight, and tears no bitterness.
Where is death's sting? Where, grave, thy victory?
I triumph still, if thou abide with me.

Henry Francis Lyte
#662, The Hymnal 1982

We know that Christ is raised and dies no more.
Embraced by death he broke its fearful hold;
And our despair he turned to blazing joy.
Alleluia!

John Brownlow Geyer
#296, The Hymnal 1982

Contents

	Acknowledgments	11
	Introduction	13
1	A Most Unlikely Possibility	17
2	This Can't Be Happening to Me!	30
3	Another Time, Another Place	43
4	Through the Valley of the Shadow of Death	51
5	The Heart Has Its Reasons	66
6	An Athlete Dying Young	76
7	Help of the Helpless	91
8	A Necessary Rest	105

9   Our Timeless Love   121

10 A Divinity That Shapes Our Ends   136

11 Coping With Life   150

12 A Change of Heart   164

13 Taking the Sting Out of Death   179

Acknowledgments

How can we adequately acknowledge and thank those whose practice of the medical arts has been a gift to us?

Dr. Walter Eichacker, who delivered our first son, Don; **Dr. Sewall Pastor,** who delivered our second son, Kevin; **Bruce and Carolyn Dodd,** who delivered our daughter, Ellyn; **Dr. John B. Lange,** who completed her delivery; **Dr. John F. Faigle,** whose care saved Ellyn as an infant; the late **Dr. John B. Mehrling,** who treated our family for many years.

Dr. George Goodman, Dr. Charles Beyrer, and the late **Dr. Arnold S. Breakey,** who together helped to restore Bruce's sight.

Dr. Frederick Silverman, in caring for Lory.

Dr. Peter F. Bruno and his team of cardiologists, who helped Bruce to survive a heart attack; **Dr. Peter F. Cohn** and his staff at the State University of New York at Stony

Brook Health Sciences Center and Hospital, who continually press forward with new discoveries to counterattack heart disease; **Dr. John P. Dervan,** whose skill in angioplasty gave Bruce a new lease on life.

Dr. David E. Weeks, whose continuing care helps to sustain us in middle age.

The Stony Brook Volunteer Fire Department Emergency Squad, led by **Kevin O'Leary,** whose prompt response preserved the life of Lory's mother, Alice Ogilvie; **Dr. Allan Cooper,** who responded when we needed a doctor to treat Alice Ogilvie's stroke.

Dr. C. Everett Koop, former Surgeon General of the United States, for his encouragement over many years.

Introduction

This is a book about a tough topic: acknowledging, sharing, then dealing with the fear of death.

It is something we have had to face in our lives. Not easy, but easier together than it would have been alone.

"In the midst of life we are in death," says *The Book of Common Prayer*. "In this world," writes Benjamin Franklin, quoting Daniel Defoe, "nothing is certain but death and taxes."

Death's coming is the inescapable fact of life: *We are all born to die.* Poets, philosophers, playwrights, and novelists have given us their vision of death. For instance, the American poet James Dickey says that "there are only two topics for poetry: the possibility of love and the inevitability of death."

So, while it may be true, as William Hazlitt claims, that no young man considers the likelihood of his own death, the subject fascinates and often troubles most thinking people at odd moments of introspection.

Those who think too deeply about death—their own or anyone else's—we label as morbid; those who never give death a thought, we charge with shallowness. What, then, is the well-balanced ideal for those of us who wish to live life to the full, yet carry with us a reasonable awareness of our own mortality?

How can we overcome the gnawing ache reminding us that, eventually, death lurks for us all? Most important, what hope can we find to help us face what Paul of Tarsus long ago called "the last enemy"?

This is a personal book, written by two people who have experienced the sudden and shocking realization that life may be shorter than we imagined. We faced this reality in the privacy of our own beings; we dealt with it together.

We make no claim to have resolved the mystery of death for anyone else. But we do believe two things to be true: First, death isn't the final end to life; second, the fear of death needn't be as suffocatingly oppressive as it once seemed.

At her death by beheading, more than four hundred years ago, Mary Stuart, Queen of Scots, spoke these words: "In my end is my beginning." For ourselves and for our readers, we hope at our own departing to be as courageous and sure.

Bruce and Lory Lockerbie
Stony Brook, New York
Winter 1990

1
A Most Unlikely Possibility

Both of them were too busy living to think of the possibilities of death.

On the surface, Lory and Bruce Lockerbie seemed like an ideal couple. At age forty-six, a pair of accomplished professionals with a home in the suburban woods and three well-adjusted and productive kids: two athletic and artistic sons recently graduated from the University of North Carolina at Chapel Hill—the older son now married to a gracious young woman he had met at college, and the younger son engaged to marry another beautiful Carolina coed; and an equally gifted daughter just finished with her junior year at the same university. A close-knit family for whom coming home meant joy in being together, good times with one another and friends.

Here was a typical American couple caught up in the hectic pace in which most people in their mid-forties find themselves—concerned about home and family, their professions, their life-style, relationships, social and political preferences, travel, recreation. Because they called themselves evangelical Christians, this couple's concerns centered on their personal faith and its evidences in service to God.

It rarely occurred to them to consider a major health problem.

They were much too young to think seriously about death. They had joked about the inevitability of the nursing home, but even that conversation was in response to discussion about their mothers, since both their fathers were deceased.

Were they so unusual?

Probably not. As it is for many couples their age, their own deaths were still something to be dealt with in the future. Although death had come near their lives, in the passing of their fathers and the near-fatal illness of their baby girl, they had survived the loss of a parent, the terror of a child's illness. They simply hadn't yet faced another possibly fatal situation. Their faith had given them an abstract comfort, a conventional reassurance concerning the Hereafter. Heaven was still a soothing thought appropriately discussed when illness or death afflicted their friends or members of their extended family.

"We're blessed," Bruce would often say, describing how wonderfully spared their lives had been from tragedy. How grateful to the Lord they were for all the goodness bestowed upon them! Were they prepared for anything else? For major illness? No better—perhaps no worse—than the average churchgoing family, whom they had heard say, "The Lord gives you the strength to bear it when your time comes."

Lory Lockerbie: married to Bruce since 1956, mother of

those three young adults, Don, Kevin, and Ellyn; a registered nurse and teacher of health education in a Long Island public elementary school; active in the Altar Guild and choir of a local Episcopal church; always supportive of her husband's administrative and professional responsibilities. Lory seemed now to have recovered well from major surgery the year before. A woman whose gift is hospitality, she had resumed her frequent hostessing of an extraordinary number of dinner and overnight guests.

Bruce Lockerbie: married to Lory, father of those same three young adults; at the time in question, dean of faculty at The Stony Brook School, a college-preparatory school on Long Island, some fifty miles from New York City; a former world-class middle-distance runner for New York University and the New York Athletic Club, now competing against his age-group in national track and road races; author of many books, with newly signed contracts for several more. As if that weren't enough, Bruce was a lay preacher at churches of all denominations; a too frequent lecturer at colleges, universities, and seminaries—earlier that spring, he'd spent five unbroken weeks on the circuit, crisscrossing the country, giving lectures from Rhode Island to Oregon; and, when at home, a choir member and lay reader in the local Episcopal church and member of the community library's board of trustees.

Lory was a self-confessed compulsive housekeeper, with one hand welded to the handle of her Hoover upright vacuum cleaner; Bruce, a sometimes irascible and nitpicking perfectionist. Outwardly, their marriage seemed placid, their children responsible; but some observers knew that the clash of Lory's Irish temper and Bruce's Scots-Canadian tenacity made for some high-tension moments and occasional thunderous quarrels. For all their efforts at covering up, almost all their friends would have agreed that the Lockerbies were then—some might insist they still *are*—a pair of driven individuals, intense about most things that mattered, obsessive about much that didn't.

Heart attack?

Of course, they knew people who had heart disease, including family members. Bruce's paternal grandfather had died of heart disease at age forty-six; for years, Bruce's father had also been afflicted. As a young man in Northern Ontario, E. A. Lockerbie had survived his first heart attack. Over the next thirty-five years, he suffered from angina and arteriosclerosis or hardening of the arteries, especially in his legs and neck. As a Baptist pastor and itinerant evangelist, he'd had three more near-fatal incidents.

A man of enormous energy and restlessness, Ernie Lockerbie had lived without apparent concern for his health, preaching with vigor and serving his congregations tirelessly. He would rather risk death than ask for help in shoveling snow off the parsonage driveway or stop a passing motorist for assistance in changing a tire. In the late sixties he'd had surgery to provide him with better circulation, but in 1973, at age fifty-nine, Ernie Lockerbie died of a cerebral hemorrhage.

But if Bruce had learned anything from his father's death, it wasn't demonstrated to Lory. As both a nurse and a teacher of health—her elementary school curriculum included study of what makes a healthy heart—she knew that Bruce's habits scarcely measured up to the standards in her lessons. While he never smoked nor drank alcohol to excess, he ate whatever he pleased. For instance, when the kids were home, Bruce presided over Sunday morning breakfasts, which usually consisted of scrambled eggs and bacon; sometimes home fried potatoes would be added. Steak was his favorite meat, with a baked potato swimming in butter and perhaps a cheese sauce. Then there was his passion for ice cream, Heavenly Hash in particular! Bruce could make a half gallon disappear while watching a football game on TV. Then the next day, he'd go out for an eight-mile run and claim to have canceled out his ice-cream binge.

The words *fat* and *cholesterol* weren't part of his vocabulary. Although Lory would occasionally rebuke—or even attack—him for these obviously horrendous eating revels, who would believe that this lean, athletic man had the same condition that appeared to be inherited from his father's side of the family? Surely he must have balanced the risk factors with the astonishingly healthy genes from his mother's family! After all, most of her strong Scottish clan all live well into their eighties and beyond.

Professionally, he lived by a schedule guaranteed to make the strongest man bend. Beyond administrative and teaching duties at The Stony Brook School, Bruce maintained a writing and speaking schedule that left acquaintances gasping. Lory lamented his frequent and extended travels, his extra-heavy suitcases, including one always packed with books to sell. She feared—correctly!—that her husband was too cheap to hire an airport skycap or hotel bellman, preferring to lug his baggage himself from the airport limousine to the hotel room and back. She had seen him, like O. J. Simpson in the car-rental commercial, literally running through airports, fretting about delayed flights, castigating desk-bound airlines personnel, who could hardly be blamed for bad weather or a faulty mechanism. Lory knew the signs were there: family history, hyperactivity, tension.

Still, she never mentioned the term *heart attack*. Even if she had, Bruce would have scoffed it away. The words just didn't apply to a man who seemed in such fit condition, who could be found each afternoon running a taxing workout and priding himself on being able to challenge most men twenty years younger than himself over distances from half a mile to ten kilometers.

During that late spring of 1982, one topic dominated all others: the Lockerbies' preparation for the marriage of their younger son, Kevin, to Kimberly May Joseph of Columbia, Maryland. The date was set for Saturday, June 19, at the Josephs' parish church in Catonsville.

Careful planning was always a hallmark of any Lockerbie family activity. For example, a decade earlier, they had taken a sabbatical leave from The Stony Brook School, traveling together as a family for nine months around the world. They visited schools for missionaries' children, where Bruce and Lory worked as educational consultants with administrators and faculty. But long before embarking from TWA terminal at Kennedy Airport—before the passports and visas were obtained, before they winced at the cholera and typhus shots—a map of the world to show their route had been spread across the kitchen wall, with all the cities on their itinerary marked and joined by connecting ribbons.

In the same spirit, while it was the Josephs' wedding to plan for their daughter, the groom's family was just as earnestly involved. Detailed preparations for gathering the Lockerbie family together had been orchestrated by the groom's father. Prior to arriving in Maryland on Friday, June 18, for the obligatory rehearsal dinner, there would be family festivities in Stony Brook, as members of the extended family began to arrive. From Long Island, a caravan would head down the New Jersey Turnpike and I-95 to Columbia, a few miles north of the Washington Beltway. Only Bruce's sister, Jeannie, a missionary in Bangladesh, would be missing from the wedding photos.

Heart attack?

Are you kidding? The thought never entered their minds. The week was filled with myriad activities. Besides family arrivals, with all the necessary trips to and from New York City airports, plus the last minute packing and checking on details with the hotel in Maryland, Bruce was deeply involved with final administrative responsibilities that surface at the end of any academic year.

With all these problems crowding his mind, Bruce struggled to complete both a graduation sermon, to be delivered across Long Island Sound in Fairfield, Connecticut, on Sunday, June 13, and an end-of-year challenge to the Stony Brook faculty, for Monday, June 14. Somehow neither address seemed to be coming together as easily as he had hoped.

For relief from such tension, Bruce went for his daily afternoon run. The week following the wedding, another important date loomed: Bruce would compete in the national championship track-and-field meet for men over forty, running the 800 meters, two laps around the track. Just two months short of his forty-seventh birthday, Bruce was still fairly lean at six feet and 150 pounds. Although 25 pounds heavier than in his competitive heyday, he was fit enough to have run in the national 10-kilometer (6.2 miles) cross-country championship race, for forty-year-olds and older, eight months earlier, finishing in fifth place.

All winter he'd run whenever roads were clear, sometimes even shoveling snow from a lane of the track, if necessary. During the spring he had competed in various open and age-group races, training daily with athletes at Stony Brook, or with his friend and neighbor Dick Wittman, another former world-class opponent from Madison Square Garden races. Bruce gloried in the fact that he was no *jogger*, a term he equated with flat-footed, balding men and lumpy women. He was and would always be a *runner*.

With two weeks to go before the national championship meet—and with wedding travel and celebration to account for—Bruce had worked out his training schedule. He would put in his last hard runs, let the wedding take place, then resume training the following week with easier workouts, tapering off to a competitive edge.

Heart attack?

Excuse us, but you're talking about the wrong people. Now, take the speaker at Stony Brook's Baccalaureate Service, Dr. Robert Cleveland Holland, pastor of Pittsburgh's Shadyside Presbyterian Church. Burdened with the responsibilities of a major church, struggling to overcome the effects of a national economic recession that had turned to a local depression, maintaining his active role in the denomination, preaching and writing constantly, Bob Holland had recently recovered from a massive heart attack that nearly took his life. Breakfasting with the Lockerbies on Monday, June 7, the day following his Baccalaureate sermon, Bob Holland's wife, Donna, had looked at Lory and said of her husband and his colleagues, "They all think they're immune."

On Monday afternoon, Bruce and Lory drove to New York City for Lory's semiannual checkup with her doctor, Frederick Silverman. Just a year before, the results of a Pap smear had indicated a diagnosis of *carcinoma in situ*, a precancerous condition. Dr. Silverman had lost no time in placing Lory in the Women's Pavilion of New York Hospital; a hysterectomy followed. Now, every six months the tests are repeated and a report from Memorial Sloan-Kettering Cancer Center eagerly awaited.

Following her checkup, Lory headed south on New York's East Side to Bloomingdale's; Bruce went across town to the New York Athletic Club on the corner of Seventh Avenue and Central Park South. While his wife displayed her credentials as a world-class shopper, the runner changed into his athletic gear and did his planned workout in Central Park. They met for dinner at the club, then returned home to Stony Brook.

The next day, however, a minor crimp appeared in the running schedule. That spring had brought an epidemic of chest colds with hacking coughs. Lory had taken two days off from school the previous week because of her disabling cough. So far, Bruce had escaped, but many others they knew were stricken.

So when Bruce went out on Tuesday afternoon, June 8, fully expecting to put in a strong five miles, he wasn't at all surprised to feel that burning high in his chest. *Here comes the same cold everybody else has,* he thought. He had covered only the first mile, but since that was a convenient point on the course to return home, he did so at a reduced pace. En route, he passed the home of Ellen Wilkens, whose late husband, Rich—a high school classmate of Bruce's—had died of a heart attack not too long before while refereeing a lacrosse match. By the time Bruce arrived home, the burning sensation had subsided.

He never mentioned it to Lory.

Wednesday afternoon brought a similar experience. The workout planned was to have been a series of five half-mile runs along a roadside with both downhill and uphill stretches: a combination of speedwork and stamina. This time, before the first half mile was completed, that same sense of burning returned, not unlike the discomfort from drinking a hot liquid too fast so that it passes painfully down the esophagus. This time, Bruce stopped running altogether and walked home, discouraged by the second day's failure to complete the workout.

On Thursday afternoon, June 10, Ellyn—a member of the Tar Heel women's track team—joined her father for a set of repeated runs along a path through the woods adjacent to their home. The distance was less than two lengths of a football field, the pace fairly easy. Yet after attempting only five of these runs, Bruce found himself unable to go on.

That evening, at the pregraduation awards ceremony, Lory and Bruce received a silver bowl marking their twenty-five years at The Stony Brook School. Sitting down after the presentation, Bruce began to feel a sense of weariness, as if a millstone were pressing on his chest.

You're getting old, Lockerbie, he told himself. *Twenty-five years in one place: That's a long time!*

Friday, June 11, was Commencement Day for The Stony Brook School. Bruce had been invited to breakfast with the day's dignitaries, the Headmaster Emeritus, Dr. Frank E. Gaebelein, and the Surgeon General of the United States, Dr. C. Everett Koop, a former trustee of the school and father of one of Bruce's favorite students, Norman, now a Presbyterian pastor in New Jersey. Both Gaebelein and Koop had been influential in shaping Bruce's career. Breakfast's conversation turned toward "Chick" Koop's efforts to lessen the risks of disease, including heart disease, attributed to smoking.

"That's one vice I don't have to worry about," Bruce told the Surgeon General. "My running has kept me from ever becoming a smoker."

Hoping to stave off the worst of his apparent oncoming cold, Bruce went home to bed immediately after the morning's graduation exercises. When Lory returned from her day at school, she found Bruce still resting. He insisted, however, that he was simply fighting off those symptoms that were becoming more apparent, especially when he was running. No need to see a doctor, he firmly asserted.

"It's just a cold, and everybody has it. What's a doctor going to tell me?" he asked with supreme assurance. "A little extra rest, and I'll be fine."

That evening, when they picked up Don and Belinda at LaGuardia Airport, Don immediately commented on how tired his father looked.

Saturday, June 12, was a busier day than Bruce could have wished. The next day's sermon and Monday's faculty address had to be completed, but a party to welcome Belinda and Don and other family members had also been planned for that evening. Midway through the morning, a call came from Frank Gaebelein, asking to be driven to his daughter's home some twenty-five miles toward New York City. At eighty-three, Gaebelein was no longer the vigorous mountaineer who had scaled some of the world's most difficult technical climbs. His heart had been weakened by several incidents before surgery.

Gaebelein had served as founding headmaster at Stony Brook for forty-one years. His retirement had been, if anything, even more stressful as coeditor of the theological journal *Christianity Today*, member of the translation team for the New International Version of the Bible, and editor of a commentary series based on that text. He had signed a contract with a publisher for a collection of his essays and, in the event of his death, had named Bruce to edit that posthumous collection.

On the way to his daughter's home, Gaebelein talked about his need to keep on working with whatever strength remained.

With those words foremost in his mind, Bruce returned and entered wholeheartedly into the festive activities of the afternoon and evening. A typical fun-filled party developed, with Bruce in good spirits, entertaining in boisterous humor. Music, laughter, and congeniality prevailed.

But around ten o'clock, Bruce excused himself, feeling very distressed. Belching and perspiring, he went to his room, wishing his guests would leave and go home. But they stayed on, so eventually he returned to the party until the guests finally departed around midnight.

Long ago, Lory and Bruce had made a pact: No party evening ends until, working together as a team, they have stacked all the dirty dishes in the dishwasher and put away all the leftovers. No matter how tired, each is obligated to the other to share in the party's aftermath. That night, however, Bruce begged off. He would be rising early to make the 6:15 A.M. ferry from Port Jefferson to Bridgeport, in time to arrive well before the service in Connecticut. Lory teased him about welching on their deal but let him go to bed.

When she entered their bedroom some time later, she found Bruce in the connecting bathroom, taking whatever remedies were at hand for what he was calling "heartburn" and other symptoms of gastric acidity.

"You're certainly not going anywhere to speak this morning!" his wife declared.

"I most certainly am! People are counting on me," the stoic replied.

"Not if you're having a gall bladder attack," the registered nurse snapped back, offering her first diagnosis.

"What do you mean, a gall bladder attack? I've just got an upset stomach."

"We'll call Dr. Mehrling in the morning."

"We can't. He retired as of Friday."

"Well, we can call his office. Somebody must be taking over for him."

"We're not calling anybody. I'll be fine. I just need to get some rest before dawn."

And he turned out the light.

2
This Can't Be Happening to Me!

I'm Bruce Lockerbie, and I'm going to pick up our story for this chapter. Lory will narrate the next chapter, and we'll alternate from there. Don't be surprised, by the way, if you find us disagreeing or one contradicting the other. As anyone who has ever served on a jury knows, recollections of a past event are often quite different, depending on whose point of view is presented. Besides, while marriage makes us one, we are two different people when it comes to how we respond or react. That's just human nature.

A peculiar thing happened that Sunday morning in June 1982.

I thought I'd be on my way to church. I arrived instead in the cardiac intensive care unit at the John T. Mather Memorial Hospital in Port Jefferson, New York.

Instead of taking the Port Jefferson–Bridgeport ferry across Long Island Sound to Connecticut, I almost took a gurney ride across the final river.

Scheduled to speak to others, I wound up doing a lot more listening than usual.

But I'm getting ahead of myself. Let me take you back to the preceding night, the worst few hours of my life.

Shortly after the steaks came off the grill, I began to feel real discomfort in the middle of my back—just about the worst case of indigestion I had ever known. To make it worse, apart from Lory's bountiful hors d'oeuvres, I hadn't eaten anything yet. I managed to fake the role of genial host for another couple of hours; then I headed for the privacy of our master bedroom and tried to throw up whatever was causing my distress. Nothing worked, so I went back to the party until the last guest finally disappeared, sometime after midnight.

At that point, I lost it! I announced that, contrary to all agreements, I wasn't staying around to help with the cleanup and, amid some hoots of displeasure by those left to do the work, took myself to bed. When Lory arrived an hour later, I was still trying to find some relief.

I knew she must be exhausted from her entertaining. Our daughter, Ellyn, daughter-in-law, Belinda, and older son, Don, had pitched in to help with the cleanup, but even so, it must have been after one o'clock in the morning when Lory entered our bedroom. The least I could do was to let her go right to sleep. After turning out the light in our bedroom, I made a determined effort to lie still and allow sleep to take over.

I knew that I had to be up by five and on the ferry dock, six miles away, by 5:45, a full half hour ahead of the first scheduled sailing time, to hold my reservation on a busy

June Sunday morning. That didn't leave much time to sleep, much less recover from whatever was ailing me.

So I tried to be calm. First, I tried concentrating on prayer, not just the many spontaneous utterances that came to mind but prayers I had memorized since, exactly six years earlier, Lory and I had been confirmed in the Episcopal Church. One of my favorites, in the service of Evening Prayer, appears in *The Book of Common Prayer* as "A Collect for Aid against Perils."

> *Lighten our darkness, we beseech thee, O Lord,*
> *and by thy great mercy defend us from all perils*
> *and dangers of this night; for the love of thy*
> *only Son, our Savior Jesus Christ. Amen.*

Much as I attempted to repeat these words, I seemed unable to hold them in memory or on my tongue. Like Macbeth, I too had most need of blessing, but "Amen" stuck in my throat. My best efforts at calm reliance on my Christian faith lasted only a few seconds.

I had never been so restless. Soon not just nervous twitching but violent writhing seized me in a vain attempt to find a comfortable position. Gall bladder, Lory had suggested earlier. Could that be what I was suffering? Or could this be kidney stones? I once heard that a kidney stone attack is God's way of informing men what it's like to go through the pains of childbirth!

Whatever it was, I couldn't endure it lying down. I tried to slip out of bed as inconspicuously as possible, but my thrashing about had kept Lory wide-awake. She turned the light back on instantly.

"I'm so restless," I told her.

"Don't I know it! Shall we go to the emergency room?"

"No, let's wait till morning and see what's what."

I had made my first concession to reality. The second came when I switched off the alarm on the clock radio, set for 5:00 A.M. With that act, I acknowledged that I would not be traveling to Connecticut to deliver that graduation sermon.

Most of the next few hours, until dawn, I spent sitting on the edge of the bed while Lory massaged the middle of my back, where the pressure seemed concentrated. Deep inside and between my shoulder blades, a special kind of torture chamber seemed open for business. Something was twisting my spine like a braided rope and sending electric shocks shooting throughout my torso and legs.

Perspiring freely, at the same time I felt chilled. Every once in a while, I'd go downstairs to the refrigerator for a sip of something fizzy—ginger ale or club soda—hoping its effervescence might dislodge the heartburn that I was sure was my sole distress. My mouth seemed parched, but nothing I drank could quench that thirst. I tried converting my belching into vomit, but all I accomplished was a racking case of dry heaves.

Once when I returned to the bedroom, I found Lory poring over one of her nursing textbooks, looking for some definitive diagnosis of my symptoms. Then the questions began.

"Do you feel any shortness of breath? Any numbness in your arms? Any pain in your chest?"

"Those are signs of a heart attack, Lory," I rebuked her. "That's what my father always had. Look up gall bladder or kidney stones."

Somehow the hours passed. At one point, I recall, the numbing pain in my spine subsided. That dull yet persistent ache, as if a great drill were slowly boring into my back, had eased. I lay back on the bed and, in pure exhaustion, fell asleep. Lory slept too.

But not for long. Something had summoned me out of sleep. Perhaps it was the first rays of sunrise already reaching over the tree line. "What is so rare as a day in June?" asked the poet. Then the gnawing returned, and I knew what had broken my brief interlude of sleep. This time I understood that something had to be done.

Lory summoned Ellyn, Don, and Belinda for a council.

"Dad's had a bad night," she told them. "I think we ought to go to the hospital."

"Can't we get Dr. Mehrling?" Don recalled the family physician of more than twenty years.

"He retired on Friday. I think he's gone on vacation."

At six o'clock on a Sunday morning in mid-June, whom do you call?

"Don't you know anyone else?" Belinda inquired reasonably.

"No."

"Then we go to the emergency room," Don decided.

"First, Dad wants you to call the pastor in Connecticut."

"Which hospital are we going to?"

We're blessed to live where medical care abounds. Just across the highway from our school campus is the State University of New York at Stony Brook, with a colossal hospital and medical school complex, serving all of eastern Long Island. Six miles in either direction, east or west, are four more private hospitals. Our family had received care in three of those five hospitals, and Don had been born in one of them.

"We'll go to Mather Hospital," he decided.

Of course, I drove us to the hospital, first stopping at a local newsstand for Sunday's mandatory copy of the *New*

York Times. Bad enough to miss church; you can't expect to make it through a Sunday without the *Times!*

At the emergency room entrance to the hospital, I took the thick copy of the newspaper under one arm and, with the other around Lory's shoulder, walked into the hospital, accompanied by Ellyn. While Belinda and Don parked the car.

A hospital emergency room is always busy on weekends, especially after midnight Friday and Saturday; but by dawn on a Sunday morning, most victims of highway wrecks have already been delivered, most incidents of domestic violence have already been resolved. The waiting area just outside Mather Hospital's emergency room was totally deserted.

Lory and I proceeded to the desk and submitted to the initial paperwork—endless questions about personal and family medical history, insurance forms, and releases of one kind or another. Just as the supervising nurse was midway through taking down her obligatory information, I had to excuse myself and find the nearest bathroom. By the time I returned to the desk, Lory had convinced the nurse to speed up her procedures and get me into an examining room.

I was wheelchaired from the waiting room into the brightly lit, sterile white area beyond a set of swinging doors. Passing through those doors, leaving behind my wife with our daughter, son, and daughter-in-law, I still had no realization that I was entering new, uncharted, and dangerous territory: the no-man's-land between life and death.

A cluster of young men and women—none of them older than my own children—stood drinking coffee and laughing together. One of the men, a curly-haired redhead wearing jeans and running shoes under his hospital garb, was recounting irreverently his most recent romantic escapade. Having failed to score with the young women in his story, he was prepared to risk his only slightly damaged ego on propositioning an attractive nurse in the group. While he raved on about his prowess with women, I sat huddled in the wheelchair. Perhaps he was merely trying to be amusing at an awkwardly early hour; somehow to me, his braggadocio seemed particularly obnoxious at that moment.

After a few more minutes of waiting, two nurses assisted me from the wheelchair and placed me on a gurney, a rolling metal cot with neither mattress nor springs, just a flat base. As soon as my position changed, from sitting in the wheelchair to lying prone on the gurney, my discomfort began again. A nurse holding a clipboard with the papers just completed in the waiting room began repeating the same questions.

"What are your symptoms? How long have you had them? Have you had these symptoms before? Is there any history of high blood pressure in your family? Diabetes? Heart disease? Stroke?"

Even as she read from the clipboard, another nurse was taking my pulse and temperature. I tried to answer as politely as possible, but I could feel my irritation beginning to bubble around the edges. The thermometer stuck under my tongue made clear responses impossible.

The interrogating nurse left me momentarily, and I heard her colleague say, "Wildly erratic pulse; 103 temp." Instantly, the entire emergency room team of nurses and doctors seemed sparked into action. A young resident doctor placed the metal ring of his stethoscope on my chest, and I quivered at its cold touch. He called for an intern to bring Adrenalin and nitroglycerin. At the same time, one nurse was hooking up a portable electrocardiograph machine, lubricating the rubber suction cups concealing their electrodes to stick on my chest and shins, running the wires back to the machine to record and chart the configurations of my heartbeat. Another nurse standing behind me began inserting oxygen tubes into my nose. A third nurse wheeled over a pole from which hung a plastic bag of clear liquid with its tube dangling. She began probing my left arm to find a blood vessel into which to insert an intravenous infusion.

When I attempted a humorous remark, the resident cut me off abruptly. "Just lie still, Mr. Lockerbie." Seeing the look of puzzlement in my eyes, he said, somewhat less sternly, "You're in very serious condition right now, and if we're going to be able to pull you through, we need your help."

I've always prided myself on being a reasonable person. Give me the facts—tell me what's what—and I can generally accommodate to the realities facing me and handle my options. I have never had much time for people who are always wishing that things, somehow, were different. Things *are* the way they *are*. Sometimes, perhaps, some things can be changed; but if not, then let's get on with the best of our alternatives. A psychologist might have a fancy term for my sort of defense mechanism against disappointment; I call it being realistic.

I have also tried to live by a simple rule: Don't presume to know more than a professional in the field. Now, that doesn't mean that I'm not assertive; I have no hesitancy at all about declaring my own mind and following its counsel. But I also try to avoid the arrogance that makes me act as though I know it all, the presumptuousness that

37

second-guesses every professional opinion and discounts every doctor's diagnosis, relying instead on my own intuition. To me, that just makes no sense at all. Yes, I want to be an informed layman; I want to ask questions and test the professional's premises and conclusions. But ultimately, I expect his or her knowledge to demonstrate its superiority over my ignorance.

Maybe that's why I've always been so utterly intolerant of incompetence anywhere I find it. I expect to hear anyone daring to speak in public use the English language precisely, accurately, effectively, even powerfully. I'm not a very kind listener if the public speaker is stumbling all over his words, hemming and hawing while wallowing in banalities and wholly forgettable remarks. I want to get up and leave!

Similarly, I expect anyone bold enough to take money for making TV repairs or hanging wallpaper or tailoring a suit to know that business and perform its skills with pride and excellence. I'm not a very patient customer if the workmanship is shoddy or incomplete.

In short, I expect everyone else to be as perfect as I am!

Admittedly, there are risks to respecting an expert's judgment and acting on that advice. I have sometimes been victimized by an unscrupulous auto mechanic who preyed on my ignorance or by a financial adviser whose competence didn't match her years of experience. But, by and large, when it comes to things about which I'm openly ignorant, I find it wisest to let those who know more than me have the freedom to act for my welfare.

This occasion, however, was an exception to my own rule. I'm not very proud of what happened in the next few moments. With oxygen tubes in my nose, an IV in my arm, and EKG attachments to my chest and legs, I nonetheless struggled to get off that cot. I fought to reclaim my authority over my own life. I had lost control of my immediate destiny, but I was determined not to be a mere spectator while other people decided my fate.

"Do you want to *die?*" the intern screamed at me. "Tie him down!"

"What do you mean, *die?*" I roared back at the medical staff, still struggling to get loose. "Let me out of here!"

The resident came to the head of the cot and leaned over so that our faces were very close. He spoke softly but firmly. "Mr. Lockerbie, you've had a heart attack, and we're trying to save your life."

"But that can't be! Your diagnosis is wrong. I'm an athlete. I'm in good shape."

If I could have done so, I would have pulled my old, mildewed scrapbooks and photo albums out of some trunk in the basement. I would have produced rusting medals from the Millrose Games in Madison Square Garden or discarded wristwatches, prizes from the Penn Relays at Franklin Field—instead of the usual clockwise numerals from one to twelve, the special face of a Penn Relays winner's watch spells out the word P-E-N-N-S-Y-L-V-A-N-I-A. I would have shown him my National Collegiate Athletic Association award for cross-country or my moth-eaten national champion's blazer and crest from the New York Athletic Club. I would also have displayed my most recent trophy, won just a few weeks earlier—proof that I was still a runner to be reckoned with, even at almost forty-seven years of age!

The resident drew back, shaking his head.

"There's nothing wrong with our diagnosis. You're lucky to be alive!"

I shivered as another blast of panic chilled me. I thought

of my friend and neighbor Rich Wilkens, struck down in his prime. I thought of David Cloos, a former student, a young physician specializing in sports medicine, who never made it back home from his morning run.

"How long will I be in here?"

"Ten days, two weeks, we'll see. It depends on how well you cooperate and how much damage has already been done."

"But I've got a wedding to go to," I pleaded. "My son's being married next Saturday."

"Mr. Lockerbie, you'll go to your grandchildren's weddings, but I'm afraid you're going to miss this one," he said.

Then the real pain began.

Not that my physical torment had actually increased; rather, what I began feeling was the pain of realizing that something large and unyielding—something solemn and intractable—had come between me and the fulfillment of my hopes. Pain caused by helplessness. Pain caused by feeling sorry for myself. And with it, pain caused by fear—specifically and for the first time, the fear of death.

With this pain also came tears of frustration, disappointment, rage. I was angry beyond all expression other than tears. Angry at my body's sudden failure; angry at myself for not having taken measures to prevent whatever had happened; angry at the bad timing of it all; angry, most of all, at God for having let me down.

Whatever happened over the next several minutes went on without protest or involvement by me. I was too stunned by the resident's announcement to do anything else but lie still and wait. But for what?

For death? For deliverance from death? For survival? A heart attack?

This can't be happening to me.
O God, this can't be happening to me!

Later, I would reflect on all these swarming emotions. At the moment, I was content to indulge in self-pity, in the anguish of knowing that I was to be prevented from fulfilling my part in the coming weekend's joys. Not only would I miss a family celebration; I might turn that planned celebration into a funeral.

I opened my eyes and realized that the area in which I was lying had been curtained off. A nurse stood nearby, her eyes fixed on the digital readouts flashing from the computerized EKG machine. Periodically a roll of graph paper ejected itself from the machine. She'd reach over and tear off a strip, read it, mark it, and record its findings on her chart.

Outside the curtain, I heard several sets of footsteps. Voices, muffled at first, became more distinct. Then a voice spoke whose message was unmistakable.

"Yeah, that's Lockerbie. It looks pretty grim."

Samuel Johnson said, "Depend upon it, sir, when a man knows he is to be hanged in a fortnight, it concentrates his mind wonderfully."

Certainly, the intern's remark took me out of my reverie and placed me nakedly in the middle of reality.

I was probably going to die.

"Can I see my wife, please?" I asked the nurse.

"In a minute, Bruce."

Bruce!

Up till then I had been *Mr. Lockerbie.*

Okay, so I'm old-fashioned, maybe even a stuffed shirt; but I hate the empty familiarity and sly anonymity of a first-names-only basis for personal identity. I hate the cozy

41

cuteness of our now-standard American greeting, "Hi, I'm Bob. I'll be your waiter." I hate the presumption that seems to entitle someone I have never met to invade my private world and take possession of my first name. I demand the right to offer that privilege only to persons of my choosing, to acquaintances-becoming-friends; I will not have it usurped by strangers.

I also dislike the obligatory put-off employed by busy people everywhere: "In a minute . . . I'll just be a minute . . . can you wait a minute?" Instead of pacifying us with false hope, why don't they tell us, frankly, *"Not now.* At some indefinite time in the yet-to-be-determined future, when all other prior and pressing necessities and unforeseen emergencies have been cared for, your request will be fulfilled"? Fat chance! The most caring nurses—I would soon discover—are drilled daily in manifold ways to stall the patient and keep him hoping. It's part of the hospital routine.

Get used to it, Bruce, I told myself. This is the Big Leagues, and so far, you're batting zero-for-everything against the medical staff.

The curtain parted, and in walked a doctor about my own age. At last, someone born before Elvis Presley!

3
Another Time, Another Place

My name is Lory.

You have met me already. I'm the registered nurse and teacher of health education who didn't recognize a heart attack, even when my own husband was having one! Am I embarrassed? *Mortified* would be more accurate.

I'm hoping to share my thoughts and feelings, still so fresh in my mind, with you in an attempt to encourage others who may experience a similar situation.

For a long time during and after Bruce's hospitalization, I had bad feelings about myself and toward him, as well as some anxiety about our future. Feelings of stupidity, guilt, anger, and fear all enveloped me, giving me a very real sense of insecurity. I went through the whole cycle, and not just once. My emotions were like a carousel, endlessly spinning me around one central reality: the fact that my husband's life was in danger. I knew that I would never again think of death as just a passage out of old age; rather, death is an ever-present reality of life.

Had I ever considered widowhood? Yes, perhaps in light conversation, when Bruce would good-humoredly joke about my dependent nature.

"Lory," he'd say, "you'll be unable to survive a month without me. I pity the next guy!"

I readily admit—even then as I laughed—that I have uneasy feelings about facing the future alone. I usually quipped back, "Well, the Lord will take me first. He knows I'd never make it on my own."

Had I ever thought seriously about the reality of losing my husband to death? I think I honestly have to say, not very often and not for very long.

Our life together had been happy. Over thirty years of knowing each other, we had both learned how to compromise and make adjustments in our very different personalities. Thirty years . . . another time, another place.

The time was 1952, the place Brooklyn, New York. We met as teenagers, when I was sixteen and Bruce almost seventeen. I was a carefree girl, raised by loving parents who indulged my brother and me in the comforts of our middle-class home. I don't remember ever being denied anything I really wanted. My parents weren't wealthy, but they seemed able to provide me with the love and security I rather took for granted as a teenager growing up in a quiet, residential section called Bay Ridge.

My father was a Roman Catholic, my mother a nominal Protestant. I remember how embarrassing this division was to me, attending Fontbonne Hall, a private, Roman Catholic, college-preparatory school for girls. Just about everyone else's parents were both Catholics, or so I thought.

My early teen years were typical, I'm sure, revolving about school, friends, clothes, movies, sports, and boys. I dated only Catholic boys, mostly because they were the ones I met through school-sponsored or parish activities. Life for me in those days was fun-filled, until the spring of 1952.

My father hadn't been feeling well for several months, although I was actually unaware of this at first. Gradually I began to overhear my parents' concerned conversations about his declining health.

My mother had begun attending a Baptist church not far from our home, and I conceded that she probably needed whatever spiritual help she was apparently receiving during those difficult months. But I recall returning from school one day and being surprised to find a visitor, whom I didn't recognize, sitting with my father. My mother seemed a bit uneasy as she introduced me to "Pastor Lockerbie, the minister of the Baptist church" she was attending. I looked questioningly at my father for reassurance. In those days, a decade before the changes brought about by Vatican II, Catholics didn't visit Protestant churches, and, more important, Catholics didn't receive spiritual counsel from Protestant ministers.

My father sensed my concern and smiled as he said, "Pastor Lockerbie and I have been enjoying a lovely visit, Lory. Perhaps you'd like to join us." I remember that afternoon so clearly; I sat with my parents and "Pastor Lockerbie," forcing myself to be polite yet wondering why my mother had invited this man to our home.

My father's illness rapidly grew worse, and he was taken to the hospital for exploratory surgery. The operation confirmed our worst fears, and my mother was informed that cancer had metastasized throughout my father's body; death was imminent. My own life was crumbling around me, and I felt a chilling panic as I wondered what would happen to us as a family.

One afternoon, while I was standing with my brother, Harry, at my father's hospital bed, Pastor Lockerbie came in and stood quietly with us. My father was drifting in and out of consciousness at this point. The Baptist minister asked if I would like him to pray. Not knowing whether I was doing the right thing or not, I said, "Yes, I think that would be fine." His prayer was very different from any I'd heard before. He seemed to be just talking to God in a very personal way, instead of reciting memorized words. Somehow I hoped that my father was able to hear him and find the peace that seemed to be with us in that room.

Death came just a few days later and, with it, the end of my carefree girlhood. I now felt a growing sense of responsibility to be more sensitive to my mother's needs, to support her in her apparent desire to attend her new church, to be more religious. Naturally, my own sense of things was that she was going through a period of grief and needed the comfort of her particular faith.

But little by little, I became aware that she wanted, even expected, me to attend a service with her. I refused even to discuss the possibility. How could she ask me to be disloyal to my father and to the religious faith he had taught me to believe was so unquestionable? My objection to my mother's new church was so inflexible, we had frequent arguments, resulting in a widening gulf between us.

One bleak Saturday afternoon, I heard my mother crying softly in her bedroom. Compassion engulfed me, and I found myself telling her that I would go to church with her the next day. She seemed so pleased that I knew God would forgive me for attending, just this once, a Protestant service.

Remember, this was 1952: Pius XII, not John Paul II, was pope. There was no spirit of ecumenical concord between Catholics and Protestants, especially Baptists, for whom— I discovered—the bias worked both ways.

Mother took my brother and me to the Sunday evening service, something utterly unknown to me. My initial reaction to the Bay Ridge Baptist Church was stony hostility. I was aware that others around us seemed to know that I was Alice Quayle's daughter—and a Roman Catholic. I felt profound guilt, just for being there. The service itself was very informal, at least by my standards, and I couldn't bring myself to participate in any of the hymn singing or prayers.

Afterwards, the pastor greeted me warmly and told me that he wanted to introduce me to his son, Bruce. I was eager to leave, but my mother lingered, talking with a few people she knew. Meanwhile, I found myself being greeted by a fairly tall, thin, nice-looking guy who said, "Hi, I'm Bruce Lockerbie."

He seemed eager to talk a bit, and I found myself saying yes to an invitation to join a group of teenagers from the church who were going to an ice-cream parlor. As we sat together in a booth that summer evening, I saw the signs of mutual attraction. We talked as though we were alone, rather than surrounded by others from the church. I learned that he was a year ahead of me in school; in fact, he had just graduated from Fort Hamilton High School, the public school a block or two away from my home, and was soon to begin his freshman year at New York University. He was quite a runner apparently—a half-miler, which meant that he ran twice around the track—and had recently taken the silver medal in the New York City high schools' championship race. His exploits had won him a full scholarship to New York University, where he'd be starting his freshman year in just a few weeks.

I was impressed! A college man!

When all the ice-cream sundaes had been consumed and the party broke up, Bruce asked if he could walk me home. I happily agreed.

The next Sunday, I went to church with my mother again, but this time the reason was to see Bruce. I hadn't heard from him during that week and was frankly surprised that he hadn't phoned. I had no idea, until I learned later, that he had wanted to call but was cautioned by his parents that the Baptist minister's son couldn't date a Catholic girl. It wouldn't be sanctioned by the parishioners, and naturally, there was a standard to uphold!

Accustomed to the Latin Mass, I found the Baptist worship service quite relaxed by comparison. The singing was actually very pleasing, and I noticed that most people really appeared to be happy to participate. For them, attending church seemed to be more than a duty. The sermon by Bruce's father wrested my attention away from trying to make eye contact with the preacher's son. I found myself actually listening to words like *salvation, atonement,* and *redemption.* It was all so new to me that I felt rather confused but happy to have something other than my father's death and my own grief to think about.

After the service, I lingered outside the church, hoping that Bruce would find me. He did, and we talked about nothing that I can recall as important, except that again he invited me to join the group going out that evening.

So began what was eventually to become the romance that would change the direction of my life.

The next few months overflowed with what seemed at the time to be tumultuous decisions for me. I wrestled with the spiritual upheaval besetting me. Was I to remain in the Roman Catholic church, or was I becoming a candidate for excommunication by slipping off to Protestant services? And, if I was truly honest with myself, why was I doing this? Was it really to comfort my mother, as I told myself in the beginning, or was it to see more of Bruce Lockerbie, who was becoming increasingly more interesting to me? At the same time I was beginning to question my own religious persuasion and what I claimed to believe as a Christian.

Not that I was some kind of pagan or unbeliever. I was a sincere Roman Catholic teenager; much to my mother's horror, I'd even given passing thought to becoming a nun. But the Baptists certainly had a different way of expressing themselves, and slowly their warmth, sincerity, and outpouring of love to my mother, my brother, and me began to soften my exterior hardness and melt the barrier I had built inside my heart.

Soon after the new school year began, I made my decision to discuss openly with Sister Mary Loyola, head of my school, my growing involvement with the Baptist church. My naïveté failed to prepare me for her reaction. She was totally unsympathetic and regarded my excursions to any Protestant church for any reason as an escapade! After trying unsuccessfully to reason with me, she took the direct course and expelled me from the school that I so dearly loved.

In a fantasy of theatrics, I envisioned myself much like a modern Joan of Arc, asserting for myself the convictions of my deepening new faith and attesting that I was certain that God wanted me to follow this new path. My Catholic friends began to think that I was more than a bit strange and couldn't understand my newfound enthusiasm for the Baptist church. I found myself increasingly left out of my social circle; as a consequence, I began to seek, more and more, the comfort of the church that was actually at the root of my problem.

Now, thirty years later, in the summer of 1982, I stood in the lounge outside the emergency room of a hospital, unable to deal with the words the nurse was speaking to me.

"Your husband has suffered a heart attack," she said kindly. "The doctors are with him now, and he'll be admitted shortly to the cardiac care unit. The cardiologist on call this morning happens to be Dr. Peter Bruno, chief of our cardiac staff. You'll be able to speak with him shortly."

My knees trembled, and I literally felt my world giving way beneath me. I looked at her blankly, rejecting the words she was uttering about a *heart attack*, challenging her version of the emergency room's diagnosis. I felt humiliated, outraged, somehow personally insulted, as she continued to repeat words such as *typical textbook picture*.

As I turned to speak with Don and the girls, my son's arm tightened around my shoulders. They had been standing not far behind me and had also heard the nurse's explanation. We looked at one another in disbelief and intense sadness. Could the timing be any worse? How were we ever to proceed with the next moments of what seemed like our shattered lives?

4
Through the Valley of the Shadow of Death

The doctor who entered my curtained cubicle was Peter F. Bruno, a respected cardiologist and chief of Mather Hospital's department of cardiology, who had drawn that weekend's duty.

Immediately Peter Bruno inspired confidence. His quiet manner, so much in contrast to the younger and more frenetic resident and intern—especially the red-haired ladies' man—at once settled me into a somewhat easier frame of mind. With his arrival the stabbing pain, like a dagger in my back, eased. I felt perfectly at rest, in spite of the gurney's lack of any comfortable mattress. In the person of this doctor, I felt sure, was someone I could reason with, someone who would get me out of there in a couple of days.

Gently, efficiently, Dr. Bruno went about his work. He studied the EKG charts and reports already available, re-

51

leasing me from having to reply yet again to most of the same questions I had already answered. If he needed first-hand information, he spoke to me in a voice that was cultured and calm. When his preliminary examination was complete, I looked up at him for a word that would dispel my nightmare and set me free to go home.

But he had only truth to tell me.

"Mr. Lockerbie, it appears you've had an acute myocardial infarction. That's the fancy term for a heart attack. I'm not going to play word games with you: This is a very serious incident. Many people in your condition might be dead before they even reach the hospital, so the fact you've made it this far is a good sign. But I want you to stop planning on any appointments in the near future. I'm afraid you'll be with us for a couple of weeks."

"Then I'm not going to make it to my son's wedding," I whined.

"No chance," the doctor replied directly. Then he added, "I'm sorry. I've got a son of my own, quite a bit younger, to be sure, but I know how much this must hurt."

At his show of compassion, my tears welled up again, but this time I kept my anger from erupting.

Dr. Bruno turned away and said something to one of the attending physicians.

"No, they don't know anything. Want me to speak to them?"

"No, I'll see them myself." Then addressing me, he said, "Mr. Lockerbie, I'm going to bring your wife and family in here to see you. I want you to pull yourself together. It'll be hard enough on your wife without adding to her burden. Tell me when you're ready."

That was the sort of challenge I needed. After all, Lory

deserved better than to see me looking any worse off than I really was.

Several long minutes elapsed before I heard a familiar clicking of heels on the hard tile floor. Dr. Bruno led Lory, Ellyn, Belinda, and Don into my curtained-off area. I tried to look composed and utterly natural, lying in a state of emergency, with oxygen tubes up my nostrils, a drip bag of medication and its IV-infusion inserted into my left forearm, and the portable EKG machine hooked up to my chest and periodically spitting out its readings.

Perhaps the doctor had warned her what to expect; perhaps her years of nursing anticipated for her. In any case, Lory never missed a beat as she came to the side of my gurney. She was smiling that wonderful, luminous smile I have come to know as her sign of encouragement, the smile that signals her full support of whatever venture we've undertaken together. From her pew in a church or college auditorium, from a bench at Chautauqua's Hall of Philosophy, I've seen that smile communicate her confidence in me and known its power to inspire me. If only that smile could work its wonders now, here, in these life-or-death conditions!

Behind her came Ellyn, Belinda, and Don, however, looking shocked at what they were seeing and not quite believing. Ellyn was biting her lower lip to keep from bursting into tears. But instantly the three young people collected themselves and joined Lory in encouraging me.

"We love you, darling," she said, her eyes glowing.

"We're praying for you, Daddy," Ellyn said bravely.

I tried to respond, but words seemed impossible to utter. In spite of my best efforts, I could feel the waves of anguish and disappointment flooding over me.

"I can't . . . the doctor says—"

"Oh, darling, Kevin and Kim will understand," Lory comforted me. "The important thing is for you to get well."

"That's the only thing that matters, Dad," said Belinda.

"Besides," Don quipped, "remember what you told me about the father of the groom being the least important person at our wedding?"

Dr. Bruno stepped forward. "I think that's all the time I can give you now, folks. We're going to take him up to CCU. After he's settled there, you can spend a little more time with him."

As she obeyed the doctor's wishes, Lory squeezed my fingertips. "See you soon, darling. I love you."

"Love you too."

"Relax and go, Dad!" said Don, as he left.

Relax and go!

I smiled at my son's sense of humor. One of my earliest discoveries as a runner had been this: The more you strain, the slower you run. The same is true in every sport. How often on a golf course we see a scrawny David drive the ball toward the horizon, while Goliath's gigantic swing merely dribbles the ball a few yards off the tee. A lithe, relaxed athlete will beat a muscle-bound gorilla almost every time. It is so important to learn to relax during a race, maintaining rhythm without tensing up; then, at the critical moment, shift gears for the final sprint to the finish line.

Relax and go! For thirty years, I had whispered those three words to myself during training runs and races; in recent years, I shouted those same three words to my Stony Brook School runners, as well as to my sons and daughter and their Tar Heel teammates at Chapel Hill. In fact, they'd heard my coaching exhortation so often, the phrase had become something of a byword in our family.

On one occasion, when both Don and Kevin were finalists in an 800-meter race, I said to them, "You know, even from my grave, you guys are going to hear me holler at you, 'Relax and go!'"

Maybe it was time to start taking some of my own advice.

On a Sunday night in June, almost twenty-seven years to the day of my own heart attack, my father had collapsed at the end of his sermon. While we were singing the closing hymn, he had motioned to me to come to the pulpit and pronounce the benediction. As I was approaching him, he slumped over in his platform chair. A young doctor in the congregation, Viggo Olsen—later a world-renowned missionary statesman and physician in Bangladesh—rushed forward and had my father carried to the pastor's study just off the platform.

While a leading deacon tried to calm the congregation and conduct a spontaneous prayer meeting, others of us crowded into Dad's study. He was placed on a reclining chair in front of his ample and well-stocked bookcases. His tie and shoes had been removed, his shirt unbuttoned. I could see that he was perspiring more than usual after his vigorous preaching. His breathing seemed to be more like gasping.

Dr. Olsen had already summoned an emergency squad from Victory Memorial, the nearest hospital. Now he was attempting to offer my father care while at the same time issuing instructions to keep the room quiet and prevent concerned and curious onlookers from crowding around their stricken pastor. He spoke with authority, in spite of the chaos around him, addressing my mother.

"Mrs. Lockerbie, where does the pastor keep his supply of nitroglycerin?"

"In the center drawer of his desk, I believe."

Standing closest to the desk, I reached over and yanked open the center drawer. Papers of one sort or another were mixed with desk supplies. Sure enough, beneath some correspondence lay a bottle of the vasodilator prescription, bearing a nearby pharmacy's label,

> *E. A. Lockerbie   Ntg*
> *One tablet under tongue every 5–10*
> *minutes if needed for chest pain.*

Empty!

"He told me just the other day that he'd run out and needed a refill," my mother spoke sadly.

"I'll run and get a refill," I said, starting out the door to the pharmacy less than two blocks up Fourth Avenue.

"It's Sunday evening," someone reminded me. "Not every drugstore is open."

"But there'll be a sign telling you where the nearest open pharmacy is."

"Go ahead, Bruce," said Harold Ericson. "I'll meet you there with my car."

In the spring of 1955, a sprint of two blocks or less was easy, even in my Sunday suit. I was in perfect shape as a nationally ranked college runner, a half-miler representing New York University and the Winged Foot of the New York Athletic Club. The following Saturday, at a race in New York City's Downing Stadium, I would face some of my toughest competitors, including Mal Whitfield, the two-time Olympic 800 meters gold medalist. If all went well, I would go on to the national championship meet, later that summer in Boulder, Colorado.

But first, the race of my life—a race against death.

I dashed from the church, heading for the drugstore at Sixty-ninth Street. As dusk turned to darkness, the Brooklyn thoroughfare was crowded with automobile traffic returning from an afternoon at Brighton Beach or Coney Island; the sidewalks were occupied by children playing hopscotch and an urban version of hand tennis, by adults sitting out on what other communities would call their lawn furniture.

I negotiated my way through them all at top speed, earning the common catcall every runner knows, "Hey, track star! Where ya goin' so fast, track star?"

Half a block before the drugstore, I could see that it was closed. But a sign in the glass door read,

In compliance with New York City ordinances, this store is closed on Sunday. In case of emergency, the nearest store open is listed below:

In dismay I read the hand-lettered name and address of the store designated to remain open. It was on Eighty-sixth Street, between Fourth and Fifth avenues. By my twenty-city-blocks-to-the-mile reckoning, that was almost two miles, there and back. I knew I could never make it in time.

But just then, Harold Ericson's car screeched to a halt beside me.

"Where to?" he called.

"Eighty-sixth between Fourth and Fifth."

We were already away from the curb.

Fourth Avenue's block-by-block stoplights showed

green all the way to the broad intersection of Eighty-sixth Street. Harold swung left and executed an illegal U-turn in front of the brightly lit drugstore. I was inside, interrupting the customer being served, producing my father's empty prescription bottle, pleading for swift action.

In moments, I had the refill and was back in the waiting car. Right-hand turns at red lights aren't allowed in New York City, but Harold Ericson made one anyway. Before he could accelerate for the return trip along Fourth Avenue, a police siren started up behind us.

"Looks like we've got an escort, Bruce," Harold said.

He slowed and waved his left hand out the window to draw the squad car alongside. The officer in the passenger seat held a revolver.

"What's the hurry?" he inquired.

"Pastor at the Baptist church has had a heart attack. We've got the medicine he needs."

"Follow close."

The siren resumed its scream and, with lights flashing, we sped back through every intersection to the church entrance. I raced inside, while Harold Ericson remained with the policemen to confirm his story for their report.

Our whole mission had taken less then ten minutes. We had even beaten the arrival of the emergency squad. I watched as Vic Olsen uncapped the bottle and administered the nitroglycerin tablet to my father. I watched as the pain eased its grip, and I thanked God for helping us all to help my father.

Then, without explanation or further cause, I spoiled the moment and trashed my own thanksgiving.

As the reality of what was happening overcame initial shock, in a mixture of anxiety and relief, I lost all composure. I burst out, verbally attacking my father for his laxity in caring for himself and his family, for his inveterate and compulsive work habits, for his driven personality, for all the characteristics that made him a prototype for stress-related heart disease. In the still overcrowded study, I was shouting at him while others looked on, stunned by my uncontrolled behavior.

Somewhere in memory I recall two things about that sorry episode: First, I recall hearing my father's voice, faintly sounding through my screaming accusations, "That's all right, son, that's all right." There I was, fool-ishly assaulting a defenseless man—perhaps, even, a dying man—bludgeoning him with my outrageous stupidity, and he was forgiving me.

Second, I remember the figure of Dr. Viggo Olsen—all six feet, six inches of him—coming at me with fire in his eyes and redirecting me forcibly into the tiny lavatory adjoining the pastor's study. "I will not have you upsetting my patient in that manner!" he told me, among other admonitions, demanding that I remain closeted until I could assure him and myself that I wouldn't interfere further with my father's care and treatment.

By this time, shame had overtaken me, shame at having exposed to church leaders and others outside our family some of the anger I felt toward my father. It was all I could do to reenter the study and face those who had witnessed my filial disloyalty and disrespect.

Now, a generation later and under similar conditions, what would my own son Kevin say to me? So much like me in disposition, as his sister and brother are like their mother, would he understand—as I had not—his father's need for work and the rewards of its accomplishment? Would he sympathize or accuse? And if he expressed his disappointment in me, would I be able to emulate my father's forgiving spirit?

Surrounded by a corps of nurses, house physicians, and orderlies, I was transferred from the emergency room to the cardiac intensive care unit in the old yet refurbished section of Mather Hospital. By this time, some of the sedating medication had begun to take effect, and I was drowsy en route to the CCU ward. Yet, as we moved through the corridor toward CCU, something about my new surroundings looked familiar. I had never been more than a visitor to others in this hospital, and certainly the current state-of-the-art cardiac intensive care equipment gave the old building a different look. Why, then, did it all seem so familiar to me?

Before placing me in a hospital bed, the orderlies removed my clothing and dressed me in one of those hospital gowns that provide neither modesty nor warmth. Then delicately, they lifted me from the gurney and settled me in the bed. After what seemed like hours on the gurney, my back had all but forgotten the luxury of a firm mattress. Leaving that rack made even a hospital bed more pleasurable than one might have expected.

All the same, I now found myself even more stuck, tubed, and tied to life-support and life-measuring devices than I had been in the emergency room. Infusions in the backs of both hands, oxygen in the nose, nitroglycerin paste on my upper arm, and the ever-present digital readout and wavelength graphing of the EKG monitor: This was modern medicine.

As soon as the nursing staff permitted, Lory came to see me briefly and alone. Don had taken Belinda and Ellyn back home. Given her stress, Lory was remarkably cheerful. Yet, how else would I have expected her to be? Without taking her for granted, I had grown to expect her consistently good-natured attitude. For years, I've told friends that my wife's most gratifying characteristic is her even temperament, her sweet constancy. Unlike her, I never had to face the problem of a mate's unwarranted mood swings; I've never returned home puzzling, "I wonder in what frame of mind I'll find Lory today?" She has always been for me the most stabilizing factor of our marriage.

"Do you know where you are?" she inquired.

"You mean, here at Mather Hospital?"

"Yes, but I mean do you recognize this part of the hospital?"

"I know it looks familiar, but with all this renovation, I'm not sure," I answered.

"This is the old maternity ward. Right here's where you came to see your first son!"

Donald Bruce Lockerbie—my namesake—had been born almost twenty-five years earlier, on a Saturday morning, October 19, 1957. How I soared with pride as I stood with my father, looking through the large nursery window, pointing in at the tiny bundle of humanity—the fruit of love between Lory and me.

Here in this very space, life had begun. Was it too much to hope that here, too, life might be sustained?

Just before she left me, Lory said, "Bruce, let's pray together."

It was our first opportunity, privately, to pray aloud. Both of us, I knew, had been praying within ourselves, but the comfort of hearing another person's voice encourages continuing prayer. So we prayed, first Lory's spontaneous prayer, asking for God's mercy upon us, then together our halting recitation of a favorite psalm, the twenty-third.

As a child, I memorized a lot of Bible passages. In those churches I frequented a generation ago, one of the marks of orthodoxy had been the surprising quantities of the King James Version many professing Christians knew from memory—knew "by heart." "Thy word have I hid in mine heart" was an injunction from the Psalmist that Christians took more seriously in those days than seems so today.

Families memorized verses from the Bible, whether around the table or on an automobile journey; Sunday school classes and youth groups competed with each other in memorization projects. More than once, I had earned a free week at summer camp by being able to recite two hundred or more verses.

But while the discipline of memorization sharpens one's mental faculties, memorizing Scripture in and of itself has no saving grace; it's of little more value than the pious recitation of rosary prayers on calloused knees while ascending the stairs of a basilica. To benefit from storing away Bible passages, one must retrieve those passages and experience the reality of their truth. The purpose of hiding the Word in my heart lies in the next clause: "that I might not sin against thee" (Psalm 119:11). Knowing the Bible by heart ought to mean living by its precepts.

The fact is that, for all my head knowledge of the Bible's promises of God's protecting and sustaining grace, I'd had only occasional personal realization of that grace in action. My prayers had been essentially immature expressions of general thanksgiving. I could make vocal sounds that resembled prayer; I could point to occasions when prayer had strengthened my resolve or given me courage to persevere or even helped me to win a race—although I now sincerely doubt that God has any favorites at the starting line.

But I had seldom really known prayer as anything more than superficial utterance. Oh, there had been other times when my own or someone else's need seemed serious enough to call for agonizing prayer: the time our infant daughter, Ellyn, was hospitalized with staphylococcal pneumonia; the time Lory had returned from her doctor with an alarming report of a precancerous condition; the time my left eye went blank with a hemorrhaged blood vessel. But even then, I had never known prayer as wrestling with God; I'd never known prayer from Job's dungheap or Jonah's steerage cabin in the whale's belly; I'd never known prayer as desperation, as hope against hope; prayer as Samson's last gasp for righteous vindication; prayer as the anonymous father's last resort, "Lord, I believe; help thou mine unbelief" (Mark 9:24).

There in the cardiac intensive care unit of a Long Island hospital, while my wife held her hands lightly to my head, the words of Psalm 23:4 took on new meaning for me:

> Yea, though I walk through the valley of the shadow
> of death, I will fear no evil for thou art with me. . . .

"Time to leave, Mrs. Lockerbie," a nurse said.

Almost before Lory was out the door, I fell asleep.

How long I slept that first afternoon, I have no idea. The sedatives and medication combined with natural physical exhaustion from the night before to overcome me. My next conscious awareness came hours later, with the return of my family and their news from other fronts. Kevin would be arriving the next day, juggling his schedule for this last week of bachelorhood to come as soon as possible; my mother would be coming from California. As for those already present, Ellyn continued to be brave, Belinda a strong woman in support of her mother-in-law, and Don mature in his sudden role as man-in-charge.

Cheering as all this was, my greatest encouragement came from the sight of my wife's beautiful countenance. Just looking at her gave me a sense of peace.

Statistics are a cold unreality until given flesh and blood. Here, as of this writing, are those cold facts, from the American Heart Association:

Annual number of heart attacks	approximately 1,500,000
Immediate deaths attributed	750,000
Dead-on-arrival—450,000	
Admitted to hospital but not surviving—300,000	
Surviving that first heart attack	750,000
Dead within the next six years from a subsequent attack—75,000	

What do these figures mean? In the United States of America, there are some 1.5 million incidents every year classified as heart attacks; that's about 4,000 heart attacks *every day*.

Of that annual 1.5 million, half will die as a result of that specific heart attack; that's 750,000 dead this year from a heart attack, 2,000 dead *today*.

Of those 750,000 dead, fully 450,000 don't even make it to the hospital. Most of them simply crumple over and die on the spot. That's something like 1,232 people who will die *today* while fighting rush-hour traffic or at their desks, on their tennis courts or while making love, watching television or in their sleep.

Among the 750,000 who survive that initial heart attack, a shocking 8 to 10 percent succumb to a subsequent attack sometime within the next six years. That's upwards of 75,000 men and women who die within six years of their first incident.

That leaves only something like 40 to 42 percent of all those who are initially stricken still alive six years later. In other words, if you're a gambler and survive your first heart attack, the odds are still against your attaining normal life expectancy.

On June 13, 1982, I had joined that first statistical group. I was now one among the 1.5 million. But, in the providence of God, I made it to the hospital. I wasn't included among the 450,000 who are DOA, dead-on-arrival. Now it remained to be seen into which other statistical batch I would fall: the 300,000 who never leave the hospital following their first attack, the 75,000 who survive an initial heart attack but only for up to six years, or the remaining 675,000 who live a full life.

During that first night, the "Code Blue" signal sounded three times over the loudspeaker in the CCU.

All three times, the medical staff made swift and strenuous effort to sustain, then revive, those cardiac patients.

All three times, they failed.

All three times, I felt a new chill of fear.

5
The Heart Has
Its Reasons

After Bruce was taken to the coronary care unit or CCU, I lingered at the hospital, while Don, Belinda, and Ellyn returned to our Stony Brook home to notify other members of the family.

First, a call to Kevin in Chapel Hill. All of us were concerned because we knew how disappointed he would be. But if anyone could break the news to him, his older brother was the right person. Only seventeen months apart in age, Don and Kevin have always been close. They had gone off to summer camp together and had been teammates at both Stony Brook and Carolina. Two years earlier, Kevin had been Don's best man at his marriage to Belinda in Greensboro, North Carolina. Next Saturday, Don would reciprocate at Kevin and Kim's wedding.

But for Bruce not to be there for Kevin's sake . . . for my sake. . . . Only Don would know how to handle the call.

Dr. Bruno appeared in the waiting room.

I will always remember the quiet confidence I felt when I saw him. I knew that he frequently saw situations similar to ours—probably on a daily basis; yet he made me feel in some way that he understood my fears and was there to help me as well as Bruce. I liked him.

I felt a need to confess my stupidity in not recognizing the textbook symptoms so apparent to the medical staff. My face reddened as I spoke, but I began to feel a reassurance as he gently led me to believe that Bruce's initial symptoms had been masked. Given the circumstances, he said to console me, I had acted in time.

Dr. Bruno's words were direct as he gave me the medical picture. The normal flow of blood through Bruce's heart had been blocked; he suspected—but couldn't confirm without further examination—that the blockage was in the left anterior descending coronary artery. How much damage had been caused by the lack of oxygen, normally supplied by the blood, to the myocardial lining wouldn't be known for some time. Bruce appeared to be responding to initial treatment, and I was given the impression that the doctor was hopeful. But neither he nor anyone else could predict a complete recovery at this time.

Dr. Bruno promised to keep me well informed and encouraged me to keep major concerns to myself.

"The most important thing now," he said, "is for your husband to rest as much as possible, without any day-to-day problems."

I knew that he was telling me, however nicely, not to worry Bruce by discussing with him the mundane matters of our hectic schedule: the wedding, our household bills, those seemingly insurmountable concerns that were flooding my thoughts.

My knees began to tremble, and I felt a tightening in my stomach as the reality of our situation hit me. Was I strong enough? More to the point, was I capable of handling these tasks on my own?

As I thanked Peter Bruno for his counsel, I turned toward the elevator that would take me to CCU. I stood silently, engulfed by others in that elevator, all sharing a common bond, yet strangers in every way. It had been more than two decades since I'd last worked as a hospital nurse; so much had changed. But now, the milieu of the hospital was once again to become a part of my life. I took a deep breath, uttered a silent prayer for courage and strength, and stepped out on the third floor and into the stark world of the medical profession.

In a sense, I was back in nursing again.

In the late fall of 1952, having transferred to the public high school quite near my home in Brooklyn, I began to think about what would be happening after graduation in June. College had always been my first consideration; however, since my father's illness and my summer experience working as a nurses' aide at a nearby hospital, the nursing profession seemed to be foremost in my mind. For obvious reasons, I also started looking into programs that would keep me in the vicinity of New York University.

After I made my decision to attend church with my mother, my life had taken on an entirely new dimension. Not only was I present for all services on Sunday, I also attended every other time the church doors were open, including a Wednesday evening prayer meeting!

One day in early October, the call I had been waiting for came. My sincerity regarding my new profession of faith must have finally passed the test of approval in the Lock-

erbie parsonage. It was Bruce asking me for a real date—
well, still not a date in the usual sense, but a runner's
version of a date: an invitation for just the two of us, the
following Saturday. He wanted me to accompany him to a
race and cheer him on while he ran for NYU's Violets.
What a wimpy name for a college team! Bruce's team
would be competing against Columbia University in something called a cross-country dual meet. Would I like to go?

Sure, why not?

Little did I know that this was the beginning of more
than thirty years of going to track meets to support, first,
my husband, then the athletes he coached, then our own
sons and daughter through their high school, college, and
club years of competition. I wish I had a nickel to spend at
Bloomingdale's for every lap of every race I've witnessed
at Madison Square Garden or at some other track. Not that
I don't enjoy the thrill of seeing someone I love sprinting
to the finish line—but all those untold other races featur-
ing somebody else's loved one!

I have never considered myself an athlete. As a teenager
I could swim and hit a tennis ball decently; lately, I've
discovered the joys and sorrows of golf. But at sixteen, my
only real interest in sports was to make conversation with
my date. I could name most of the Brooklyn Dodgers, one
of whom lived just up the street from my house. Beyond
this, I knew next to nothing.

I told Bruce that I would be happy to go with him; I also
explained that I didn't know anything about his sport of
running. Bruce met me early on Saturday morning for our
two-hour subway ride—literally from one end of the line
in Brooklyn to the other end in the Bronx. He must have
worried about how I would react to my first experience as
a spectator at a race. Among his personality quirks the first

one I discovered is Bruce's need to be sure that everyone understands all the reasons behind what we intend to do. He's the kind of person who expects everyone else to be fully informed and remember, down to the smallest detail, whatever it is he has told them. Sometimes an irritating trait, let me add.

Well, on this particular Saturday morning, he spent much of our long subway ride explaining to me the whos and whats of his sport of running. The 1952 Olympic Games had just been held during the summer in Helsinki, Finland, and he was full of names and details I'd paid no attention to at the time. None of his talk meant anything to me, but I tried to appear interested because he was so interested. Then he began to describe something called cross-country.

He told me that, in the fall, the sport of running leaves the oval track and goes to parks and golf courses, where runners follow a trail for three or four or even six miles. Van Cortlandt Park, at the northernmost tip of New York City, is one of the major sites for cross-country racing. During the Revolutionary War, General George Washington had used what is now the park to marshal his troops for the defense of New York against the British. Now, on a typical Saturday morning, September through December, thousands of high school runners and hundreds of college and club athletes compete in a different kind of war, race after race. By the time we got off the train at Broadway and 242nd Street, he had the sport all built up in my mind like a marine corps obstacle course.

Ordinarily, Bruce would have gone to the NYU gym to meet his coach, an old man named Emil Von Elling, and his teammates; after dressing for the race, the team would be transported to Van Cortlandt Park. But on this important occasion, he wanted to impress me, I guess, so he had arranged to meet his team at the park. When we got off at the last subway stop, he went to a locker room on the edge of the park and changed his clothes. A few minutes later, he emerged, wearing his deep purple NYU colors and carrying his newly imported German spiked shoes by Adidas, and we were on our way to the starting line alongside Broadway, where I expected to see mountains like the Alps for these poor runners to climb.

Instead, I saw a field flat as a table. Acres and acres of nothing but flat playing fields. Off in the distance, to be sure, were some hills, but the whole impression I had received, of toughened runners skimming up and down the inclines of steep ravines, had been slightly overstated. What a letdown! I must have said something to that effect, because the next thing I knew, Bruce had me walking across those flat fields toward the hills.

I have now become a fast walker, but in those days I was rather leisurely about exercise. He led me through a bridle path to a point where the hills really did become quite steep. He began jogging and running ahead of me, then walking back to join me—"warming up," he called it— and we continued through the wooded trails. From time to time, I noticed, he would check his wristwatch. At one point, Bruce suggested a shortcut so that he could get back to the starting area in time for his race.

As we reached a place where the woods opened upon a picnic area and a bridge crossed the highway below, a group of runners was approaching. I heard my date cry out, "Oh, no!" There, just finishing the first mile of their five-mile stint, was the pack of purple-shirted and light blue-vested runners.

"Nice goin', Lockerbie," one of them grunted as the pack passed by.

My hero, the college athlete, had missed his race. With very little aplomb, he took off for the starting area, calling back over his shoulder, "Follow me!" How he expected me to keep up with his pace or find my own way out of the woods and back to civilization, I have no idea. All I know is that he was scared of his coach, scared he would lose his scholarship, and that was more important at the moment than gallantry.

Our ride back to Brooklyn that Saturday afternoon was quite subdued. Bruce had been made to run twice the distance of the race he'd missed. That left me with a lot of time to contemplate the autumn leaves. It also left him sleepy for our subway ride home. On a scale of one to ten, I considered our date to have been a zero.

Bruce survived his freshman error and eventually made his way back into the good graces of Coach Von Elling, mostly on the strength of his development into a nationally ranked competitor. But as for me, over the next four years, whenever I saw Emil Von Elling, I had the feeling that he considered me a loose woman, a distraction to his half-miler.

After Bruce recovered from the humiliation of our first date, he phoned again. We began to see each other frequently after that, and ever so subtly those initial feelings of attraction began to change, almost without our knowing it. I remember, one day, suddenly awakening to the realization that I was in love.

In the fall of 1953, I entered the School of Nursing at Methodist Hospital in downtown Brooklyn. Throughout the following years, Bruce and I increased the intensity of our relationship from "going steady" to courtship and engagement. As I looked forward to completing the final year of my student nursing experience, we began to talk seriously about marriage. I was surprised to learn a story Bruce still loves to tell: "Lory, my father picked you out for me. Remember the day he visited with you and your parents, just before your dad died? Well, he came home that afternoon and told me, 'Bruce, I've met the girl you're going to marry!' "

I was barely twenty years old, but I was confident that nursing studies had prepared me in a unique way for marriage and a family. Looking back now, I'm not so sure.

Following graduation from New York University, Bruce enrolled as a graduate student at Wheaton College, in Illinois, teaching Freshman English and assisting his idol, Gil Dodds, the one-time holder of the world's indoor mile record, in coaching the track team. I remained in New York, preparing for my exams to become a registered nurse. We were to be married on December 15, 1956.

A nurse about my age came through the wide doors of the cardiac care unit. Just for an instant before the doors closed again, I caught a glimpse of the space beyond. Somehow it looked familiar, but at the same time, its very newness terrified me. A lot had changed in the years since I worked as a registered nurse. The equipment was either updated or altogether new; I was well aware of my ignorance in the modern technologies of a CCU.

"You can go in now, Mrs. Lockerbie," the nurse told me, "but just for a few minutes."

"Thanks," I answered, wondering what the next few hours would mean for me. I felt as though I were at a crucial turning point. There could be no glancing back, only straight ahead. Here, facing me, was the man I loved, looking to me for strength and encouragement.

Would I pass the test?

The first twenty-four hours following a heart attack are always the worst.

For medical reasons, those initial hours of care are the most critical period following any cardiovascular incident—whether it's a myocardial infarction or a stroke or some other attack. That is the time when most of the initial damage either comes under control or else, at the very least, leaves the patient in danger of some permanent affliction. That's also the time when medical science discovers whatever damage can be reversed and, if possible, reclaimed to health. But if the initial damage is severe enough, the event proceeds to take the patient's life.

As a nurse, I knew the meaning of the words *intensive care*. Even so, I was unprepared for what I saw when I first stepped into Bruce's room. Whatever outside chances I had been clinging to—that this was only a bad dream from which I'd soon awaken, and everything would be back to normal—those fantasies disappeared the moment I saw Bruce and realized that he was in a precarious state.

I hadn't told anyone that I'm an R.N., but just from observing the three women on duty and the way in which they were keeping a constant revolving watch on his monitors and recording his vital signs, I knew this was no ordinary care. During one of the brief intervals when we were alone in the room, I checked his chart on the clipboard at the end of his bed. I recognized the nurses' entries as typical for a patient whose condition would be termed "critical" at this stage.

Reading those words brought home to me the reality of where I was and why. I'm not usually a panicky person.

From my years of hospital nursing, I knew I could remain cool under pressure. But I must admit that this poise had been in professional dealings with patients outside my own family. Here was an entirely different experience, and I didn't feel very cool. In fact, I felt again as though I were living through some nightmare; I would wake up any minute and find that the weight so heavy upon me had gone away.

Bruce looked so pale and exhausted. He was sleeping a sleep induced primarily by the combination of medications; he seemed to have aged a decade and more in appearance. I could feel tears welling up within me. Still possessing enough common sense not to want him to waken and see me as a pitiful creature, I sat down quietly by his bedside and closed my eyes.

I don't know how long I remained in this state, half praying, half thinking, barely aware of anything at all. Slowly, I began to focus on what thousands of people deal with every day. I thought about death and what it means to the person facing it, to me at that moment. I knew that I believed in eternal life, but I didn't find it very comforting at that instant. All I knew was that I was terribly frightened, afraid of losing the man who was the center of my life.

Just then, I must have opened my eyes to make sure he was still breathing. As I looked at him, Bruce too must have sensed my being there. I felt his hand, almost immobile with infusions, trying to move toward mine.

As he touched me lightly, he whispered "I love you, Lory."

6

An Athlete
Dying Young

I awoke after that first night in the hospital, enveloped
by fear, fixated by my surroundings and their presumed
proximity to the morgue, the hearse, the cemetery, The
End. The promises of Psalm 23 seemed to have evaporated, replaced by the noxious presence of death.

For most of the night, I hadn't slept except for brief
periods of dozing. Three times during the night and early
morning I listened and watched as the Code Blue signal
sounded, sending nurses and doctors into last-ditch hero-
ics to save their patients. Three times the rolling stretcher
bearing a body bag had been pushed past my room where,
propped up at a forty-five-degree angle, I stared out
through the windowpane in the door into the dimness of
the CCU's work area.

For most of the interim between each episode, I was
wholly occupied with studying the increased likelihood of

my own demise. On an overhead shelf to my right, the EKG screen, showing its green digital figures and waves, recorded every rapid and erratic pulse, every skipped beat, every speedup caused by my habit of crossing my ankles or trying to stretch my arms behind my head—all but impossible now, with an IV in each hand. Any slight physical movement—even any rise in my level of anxiety—showed accelerated and unstable consequences.

As those ghastly hours inched by, the EKG readings fascinated me. My normal pulse rate had been 52 beats per minute; now the liquid crystal display was producing numbers ranging between 145 and 180. Lying idle in bed, my heart was pumping as wildly as if I were in the final stages of exhaustion at the close of a competitive six-mile run.

The graphs measuring the heart's contracting and relaxing as it struggled to do its work looked just as erratic. Instead of tracing a steady pattern of peaks and valleys, as in a healthy heart, these graphs seemed like the awkward scrawls of a crayon-wielding toddler—irregular and asymmetrical.

Although I had no medical training and no technical expertise at reading an EKG, I understood just enough of what I saw to frighten me. Yet I couldn't seem to turn away from watching. In my agitation, I wished to regain some control over my condition. I tried regulating the pulse rate by an act of my own will. Holding my breath for a few seconds seemed to reduce the heart's pace; but when I took the next needed breath, it sped up again. I stopped trying to influence my pulse and simply stared at the machine.

From time to time throughout the night, a nurse would come to look at the machine, take its readings, check the dripping fluids, offer me a urinal bedpan, or administer more nitroglycerin paste, whose side effect was to produce vise-lock headaches. Each time she came to my bedside, it seemed, another corpse had been wheeled away. But when I inquired about the Code Blue emergency or asked for the condition of the patient, she ignored my questions and their implications, cautioning me not to concern myself with other people's situations.

"You've got enough to do, just taking care of yourself," she warned.

After the third patient's death, however, the nurse came in with a paper cup containing a capsule.

"You need your beauty sleep, Bruce. I'm giving you a Valium to help you relax."

As she left my room, she shoved something like a screen or room divider in front of the window in my door. Thereafter, I slept deeply, until awakened by the arrival of the morning nursing staff.

Attempting to cover my fear with humor, I said to my new nurse, "Now I know why they call that crew you just replaced 'the graveyard shift.' "

This nurse gave me her we-are-not-amused look and said nothing. Instead, she took out a huge syringe like a stiletto and began making what looked to me like threatening gestures.

"Bruce, we're going to start giving you a drug called Heparin. It's injected into your abdomen."

"Where?" I protested, in spite of how the EKG might have reacted.

"It sounds worse than it really is. Pull up your gown."

This lady meant business. Before I could quiver or tense up in unpleasant anticipation, she struck with that needle, injected its contents, and withdrew it. This was the first of several doses daily. For weeks to come I would carry a purple-and-yellow bruise on my belly to remind me of Sally Roberts's no-nonsense nursing care.

"See, Bruce, what did I tell you? Nothing to it. Besides, after what you've gone through, you can stand anything, right?"

As days elapsed, I grew to admire Sally Roberts and her cheerful spirit. She was a woman with a mission. She believed that most of her patients held within themselves the faculties to determine whether or not they would survive and recover their health: willpower and good humor, yes, but also transcendent faith. Her own role was merely to make such survival and recovery more likely.

Sally Roberts moved through that CCU with such ebullience, that only the most despairing and self-pitying among us could have failed to respond to her brightness of spirit. She would not tolerate expressions of gloom without an attempt at an uplifting rejoinder. She was all business, utterly professional, never intrusive into personal matters nor obtrusive during family visits; and as I got to know her better, something else: I learned that she was a believer whose Christian faith was the source of her continuing joy and hope.

But on that first morning, I felt no joy and hope myself. I can't even claim to have awakened with thanks for still being alive. I had witnessed three other cardiac patients dying in one night! That was more than venturing into the valley of the shadow; it was like lingering in a charnel house. I felt like a prisoner confined to Death Row and awaiting my turn in the chamber of horrors.

Fear, rage, helplessness—these were my sentiments. Not the spiritual virtues, not the fruit of the Spirit. Fear that something very precious was being taken from me;

fear that life's golden elixir had already begun to seep away; fear that, whatever my few accomplishments might have been, they'd be left incomplete and essentially worthless; fear that there would be no tomorrow.

Which led to rage. No, that's too fancy a word. The reality is that I was mad, very mad! Angry at myself and my body for its weakness, but most of all, angry at God for failing to sustain me. Anger such as this goes far beyond any ill temper toward another human being, for in our worst moments we can always think of some wicked scheme by which to get even, get revenge against the person who has offended us. But how do you get even with God? How do you make God pay for His part in your suffering?

Which led to helplessness, an overwhelming sense of frustration at my inability to do anything whatever to help myself or anyone else. At times, I couldn't even think, never mind respond or act. I saw myself as a victim of fate, a loser in the genetic lottery: a son in a paternal family line, all of whose men, as far back as our genealogies could trace—including my own father—had died by age fifty-nine. What more was there to do than lie still and wait for that inevitable inheritance to come my way as well?

So I indulged myself in a morass of despondency, certain that when the next Code Blue sounded, its Klaxon would be for me.

By midmorning, Dr. Bruno had made his rounds, bringing with him members of his cardiology staff.

"We want to ask you some more questions, Bruce, to clear up some ambiguities in your case. But we don't want to weary you, so be sure to let us know when you begin to feel tired."

I assured him that I was ready to be interrogated.

He took from his clipboard a piece of blank paper and drew an irregular shape, not at all like a Valentine's Day version of the heart.

"Do you know how the heart's divided into left and right chambers?" he asked.

Foolishly, I nodded, disclaiming my true ignorance of my body's most important organ. Later, I would summon the humility to ask my wife to explain to me what she teaches her elementary school children: how the heart functions like a pump, receiving the body's blood supply into the right upper chamber or atrium, passing it into the lower chamber, the right ventricle; then on to the lungs to receive its necessary oxygen; from the lungs, back to the left atrium and down into the left ventricle, from which the blood is pumped through the aorta to the whole body.

"Your EKG readings confirm our preliminary diagnosis. You did have a bona fide myocardial infarction or *m-i*, as we call it. You've probably sustained some permanent damage to heart tissue here," pointing to the myocardium. "Furthermore, it seems clear to us that your *m-i* has been progressive rather than sudden. Just exactly what caused it, we can only speculate at this time. We'd have to do an angiogram to learn precisely which arteries are blocked and how badly."

Angiogram! My teeth chattered at the word. All I knew about that procedure I had learned from my father's experience, a dozen years earlier. Dad had been chosen by a team of cardiologists at New York University Medical School for experimental surgery to correct the arterial blockages that continued to weaken him. But to discover the precise location of these fatty tissues impeding the flow of blood, Dad had been given two angiograms. Under local anesthesia, a catheter is inserted through a major blood vessel—usually in the groin, sometimes in the upper arm—and pushed through the body until it reaches the point of blockage. There an X-ray machine can show the medical staff exactly where the vessel narrows so badly that circulation slows and the rest of the body suffers.

Dad's angiograms had shown that, in the area of his collarbone, a section of his aorta—the major artery carrying the blood supply from the heart to the rest of the body—had been blocked by plaque. It needed to be reopened or replaced by a whole vessel from his leg.

But for some reason these angiograms had not gone well; or, perhaps, my father's level of tolerance was lower than normal. In any case, when a third angiogram was announced, my father jumped off the stretcher taking him to the surgical theater, went back to his room, and demanded to be released. We were called to consult with the doctors, to calm Dad and encourage him to go forward with the corrective surgery. He agreed, provided that there would be no more angiograms.

No doubt, that surgery had added some years and relief from discomfort to his life; it would have been impossible, however, apart from the information obtained by the angiogram procedure. But according to Dad's later description, the surgery itself was nothing compared to those dreadful angiograms!

So when I heard Dr. Bruno talk casually of performing the same torture on me, I silently resisted.

"Of course, the same is true for coronary bypass surgery," the doctor continued. "We wouldn't consider that until we'd examined you by angiography."

I shivered again at the thought of a wire being shoved through my veins. I could imagine it scraping its route inside me. I resolved that there would be no angiogram for me.

"But before we go any further, we need to know more about the symptoms that brought you here yesterday morning. How long had you been experiencing angina?"

I had never heard that word pronounced with stress upon its first syllable, its middle vowel short rather than long: *AN-gin-a*, rather than *an-GY-na*. *You learn something every day*, I thought.

"I'd never experienced angina," I repeated the doctor's professionally correct pronunciation, "before last Tuesday." I explained my burning chest pain while running and its supposed connection with the series of summer colds in our community.

"Tell us about your running," one of Dr. Bruno's associates asked. "Do you jog every day?"

The speaker was a squat, rotund fellow, maybe a former handball player, possibly a former swimmer, but obviously no longer a frequent visitor to any exercise venue.

"I'm no jogger," I retorted unpleasantly. "I'm a runner. There's a big difference. Fashion plates and dieters *jog;* athletes *run.*"

"So, tell us about your *running,*" he replied, more good-naturedly than I deserved.

As my father recuperated at home from that Sunday evening heart attack in 1955, so my wounded ego had struggled to recuperate from its shame. I had humiliated him and my mother by my stupid outburst in his study, venting my anxiety in fury against him; I'd earned the public rebuke of Dr. Viggo Olsen and probably the contempt of others in the church. Now I needed some way of making amends.

Unlike my mother, my father's interest in my running had always been more promotional than athletic. From my earliest endeavors as an elementary school sprinter, Jeanette Lockerbie seemed to grasp the details of my sport. She was both my staunchest fan and my sternest critic.

When my high school's athletic budget lacked sufficient funds to send our one-mile relay team to the Penn Relays in Philadelphia, it was she who stood up at a PTA meeting and asked for the parents to donate the money. It was my mother who drove me a thousand miles round-trip, through a February blizzard, so that I could compete in and win a Canadian national championship race. It was she who drove four of my NYU teammates and me to a meet in Massachusetts. We won the relay race that day and presented Jeanette Lockerbie with the trophy. And when our car got stuck in a Manhattan traffic jam and I had to run to make a train at Grand Central Station, it was Mother who flew to Michigan with my running gear, left behind in the trunk of that gridlocked car. I probably owe her the NCAA bronze medal that her ingenuity and dedication made possible.

But Mother was also tough to live with when I didn't win. She wanted nothing but the best on every occasion, even in a preliminary race called a "trial heat," in which the runner's only objective is to qualify for the final race. Never mind conserving energy; Mother wanted me to win both the heats and finals.

"You shouldn't let that Villanova runner think he can beat you so easily," she'd warn. "If he beats you in the heats, he begins to believe he can beat you in the finals." Who could argue with such logic?

My father was more pragmatic. As far as he was concerned, what counted was the distribution of prizes and the write-up in Sunday's papers. He never really understood the sport, didn't know precise lap times or race strategy the way Mother did; but he relished the publicity that accompanied his son's success on the track. When Jesse Abramson of the *Herald-Tribune* or Barney Kremenko of the *Journal-American* or some other New York City newspaperman wrote about "the Baptist preacher's kid" on NYU's track team, my father would find a way to work it into his morning sermon!

On the Saturday following Dad's heart attack, I was listed to run 800 meters in the Metropolitan track and field championship meet, a prelude to the national championships, later that summer. Wearing the New York Athletic Club's Winged Foot colors, I would go to the starting line against the most challenging field I'd yet faced. Scheduled to compete were collegiate, national, and international middle-distance stars, including the 1948 and 1952 Olympic champion, Mal Whitfield.

But my training that week was listless. I kept thinking back to Sunday night. Yes, I had won a race-against-death for nitroglycerin, but still haunting me was my foolish display of petulance. I found it impossible to forgive myself for attacking my father when he was down. I recognized that, under the guise of letting him rest, I avoided visiting his bedroom whenever possible.

On Friday afternoon, the day before my big race, I returned home from a light workout and heard Dad calling me to his room.

"Tomorrow's the Metropolitan meet, right?"

"Yes, sir."

"Feeling ready to take on the field?"

"I'll do okay, I guess."

"You know, son," my father said, "I've been reading

the Epistle to the Romans this week, and I just came on a verse I'd like you to take with you tomorrow. It's here in chapter 9, verse 16," and he handed me his well-worn Bible.

I read the Apostle's case for God's sovereignty:

> So then it is not of him that willeth nor of him that runneth, but of God that sheweth mercy.

"See, Bruce, it's not entirely up to you how the race turns out. God has something to do with whether we win or lose, live or die. What matters is that we're submissive to His will and accept it as His mercy. I know that now, better than ever."

I gulped back the emotion that rose in me, reached out and took his hand, and said, "Thanks, Dad."

Late the following afternoon, I returned home from Randall's Island stadium in New York City and presented my father with the gold medal for my 800-meter victory over some of the best runners in the world.

I had experienced firsthand God's mercy in my race. Could I also hope for God's mercy in my father's illness?

All that had been twenty-seven years earlier. Now, lying in my own hospital bed, I had no such assurance of God's mercy. Whatever marginal prospects I held out were self-impelled, drawn from a disciplined will and a personality marked by relentless tenacity.

So, in answer to Dr. Bruno's associate, I provided a brief history of my athletic career, as if the very act of rehearsing its highlights could somehow restore the strength that had once earned me world ranking. Yet, even as I was speaking, a stanza of a familiar poem taunted me. The lines are from A. E. Housman's "To an Athlete Dying Young," an ironic tribute to a runner whose early death comes only in time to spare him from obscurity, for his victories are still recent enough to be remembered and treasured. The poet writes,

Now you will not swell the rout
Of lads who wore their honors out;
Runners whom renown outran,
And the name died before the man.

The doctors were understandably less interested than I in my imaginary scrapbook of major races. They could already perceive all they needed to know about this patient, simply from his asperity, his agitation, his intensity. I was—I'd been—a runner who took his running too seriously, who invested too much of his own sense of self-worth in the results of a footrace: the place of finish, the time and its relationship to improvement or failure to reach a new personal best. I had long ago lost the sporting concept in my running and turned it, instead, into my own version of warfare, a combative way of promoting self-interest.

What's more, as both a coach and father of athletes, I sometimes behaved in much the same manner. Not unlike those parents of Little League baseball players whose ego-involvement in their children's performance is often a cause for scandal, I too had stormed the sidelines when an official decision went against my team; I had berated track-meet officials for their lack of knowledge of the sport and embarrassed my own sons and daughter by my arrogance and insistence on matters of policy and organization. I had lost perspective on the sport as a means of physical exercise, competitive enjoyment, and step-by-step character building; instead I'd made it a means of gratifying my baser instincts, a tribute to my less worthy motives.

Now, it seemed, I was going to die, killed in part by the very thing I most adored.

"Well, Bruce," Dr. Bruno spoke, "it's certainly clear to us, from a preliminary consideration of your case, that you're a very intense individual. Your wife has told me something of the schedule you keep. If you pull through—and we think that's likely—you're facing some major changes in life-style and diet and attitude."

If you pull through—and we think that's likely . . .

Words intended to encourage. Yet I heard more clearly the second part of the doctor's remark: *you're facing some major changes. . . .*

And what if I didn't want to change? What if I didn't want to give up my hard-driving life, my many responsibilities; most of all, my running?

"I'll see you again later on," Dr. Bruno said as he and his team left.

Outside my room, I heard a familiar step, then the sound of voices I knew, and through them all, Lory's voice introducing the cardiologist to Kevin, who had arrived that morning from North Carolina, and my mother from California. I trembled, anticipating a sorrowful conversation with my younger son.

Then they were all in the room, including my mother, fresh off the red-eye flight from Los Angeles. Kevin hung back and greeted me last. In his eyes I saw all the love and understanding I wished I had shown my own father.

"I'm so sorry, Kev . . . ," I attempted to speak.

"You don't have to say anything, Dad. Kim and I just want you to get well."

Soon Sally Roberts appeared at the door with our Episcopal parish priest, the Reverend Canon Paul F. Wancura,
rector of the Caroline Church of Brookhaven in our neighboring village of Setauket.

"You can't all stay," the nurse addressed my family.
"After all, this isn't the Last Rites."

Among them, Lory and my mother were designated to
remain while our rector offered the service of Ministration
to the Sick. Canon Wancura read, first, from Psalm 91 (vv.
1, 15),

> He that dwelleth in the secret place of the most High
> shall abide under the shadow of the Almighty. . . .
> He shall call upon me, and I will answer him: I will
> be with him in trouble. . . .

Then from the Epistle of James (5:14, 15),

> Is any sick among you? let him call for the elders of
> the church; and let them pray over him, anointing
> him with oil in the name of the Lord: And the prayer
> of faith shall save the sick, and the Lord shall raise
> him up. . . .

Finally, from John's Gospel (6:47),

> Verily, verily, I say unto you, He that believeth on me
> hath everlasting life.

Together, we prayed the Prayer of General Confession,

> Most merciful God, we confess that we have sinned
> against you in thought, word, and deed, by what we
> have done, and by what we have left undone. . . .

89

and received the promise of forgiveness. Then the rector opened a small container of oil, sanctifying it with prayer, and placing both hands on my head, making a thumbprint of oil on my forehead in the sign of the Cross, while saying,

> I lay my hands upon you in the Name of our Lord and Saviour Jesus Christ, beseeching Him to uphold you and fill you with His grace, that you may know the healing power of His love. Amen.

Before celebrating Holy Communion, Canon Wancura prayed again,

> The Almighty Lord, who is a strong tower to all who put their trust in Him, to whom all things in heaven, on earth, and under the earth bow and obey: Be now and evermore your defense, and make you know and feel that the only Name under heaven given for health and salvation is the Name of our Lord Jesus Christ.

To which we all replied, "Amen."

In those solemn moments of prayer and penitence, just before receiving the wafer on my tongue, a sudden rush of believing faith swept over me. Unbidden, undeserved, a true gift.

Whether I lived or died would not be entirely up to me. It would depend on many factors, all under God's sovereignty, all subject to God's mercy.

By faith, I knew that to be an immutable truth.

Now, could I—again by faith—claim that trust as a sure promise?

7
Help of the Helpless

When someone very close to you looks death straight in the eye, you too experience it in a small way.

When a loved one's illness takes center stage, the habits of business and domestic chores are all set aside; a new schedule takes over. My school principal responded immediately to my call for help, and the final two weeks of health classes were covered without my giving them another thought. As for household tasks and even my wedding preparations, all those were instantly discarded.

In their place, my life now revolved around trips to the hospital. The cardiac care unit became familiar territory, whereas my world at home seemed as distorted as a Salvador Dali landscape. Nothing held the same shape as before; nothing seemed real. I sometimes wandered from room to room, bewildered by anxiety. A few hours earlier, our home had been alive with gaiety; now my deepest joy was threatened.

Sunday evening's visit had been particularly stressful. Bruce drifted in and out of consciousness, sedated by medication but also weary from the struggle to live. He was passive now, like a man tired of fighting the medical attention and finally grateful for it. Well into that evening, I sat with him. Leaving that night was one of the hardest things I've ever had to do—not knowing if he would still be there when I returned the next morning.

But even in distress there were simple causes for thanksgiving. Just a year before, Bruce had been driving daily the hundred-mile round-trip through Long Island's traffic congestion to visit me at New York Hospital in Manhattan. At least I didn't have that trip to concern me. Port Jefferson was only an easy six miles from home.

Don, Belinda, and Ellyn were wonderfully supportive, Don answering the phone; the girls taking care of the household routines. I'd like to claim that I spent those hours in meditation and prayer, but the truth is I spent them in a daze. Every time I tried to pray, fear of Bruce's death blocked my attempt.

Soon after Dr. Bruno had first told me that my husband had been stricken by a heart attack, I called our school chaplain and assistant headmaster, the Reverend Peter K. Haile, a friend of more than twenty years. He came to visit with me at our home.

A former runner himself at Oxford—a teammate of Roger Bannister—Peter Haile knows my husband and all his foibles as well as anyone outside the family. He listened kindly as I expressed my emotions—shock, anger, fear, helplessness. Then Peter prayed with me, asking God to give me peace.

When he finished praying, Peter and I remarked on the fact that, just a year before, he and his wife, Jane, had come to the Women's Pavilion of New York Hospital to visit me at the time of my surgery.

"The Lord seems to be saying to both of you, 'Slow down, rest, trust Me,' " Peter said. "Nobody can keep up the pace that Bruce set for himself this spring."

After Peter left, I thought about what he had said and knew that he'd spoken kindly and truthfully. *Rest.* Bruce and I both needed to take a break and learn something about resting as a means of restoring lost strength.

He restoreth my soul.

These words from Psalm 23 came easily to my mind, but they took on a new meaning that day. Somehow I felt they had been written just for me. A fresh warmth filled me as I read and reread those words. My spirit grew calmer and I could sense the horrible grip of fear being broken—or was I myself letting go of the fear to which I'd been holding on?

Could I change things? No, of course not, but I obtained a new strength in accepting the situation. For the first time, I knew it wasn't my burden alone, and the quiet voice within me kept giving me the words of comfort I needed: *I will never leave you nor forsake you.*

By the time we returned to the hospital the next morning, Kevin had arrived, along with Bruce's mother. Having lived her entire married life with the threats and repeated instances of her own husband's heart attacks, she knew better than anyone else what anguish I was going through.

For my part, I hoped I would be sufficiently prepared to find my husband tied to life-supporting technology, but stepping into his room and finding him so helpless still shocked me.

As we arrived at the door of Bruce's room, Dr. Bruno and his team were emerging. My own heart stopped for a moment, but then I saw his reassuring look.

"We're pleased with your husband's progress," he told me, including the rest of the family in his glances. "As you know, these first twenty-four hours are critical, but his condition appears to have stabilized, and there's reason to feel that, if it continues to improve, he's going to pull through."

The doctor went on to tell us that he didn't yet know the full extent of the damage, but all that information would come later.

"For now, it's essential for your husband to rest, free from worry, and let his heart begin the healing process."

Looking around at the family group, Dr. Bruno added, "That means staying away from conversation that might lead to any disagreement or agitation. Can you all do that?"

"We can if he can!" Don spoke for us all.

We were informed that Bruce would stay in the hospital for a minimum of two, possibly three, weeks; then he'd be given a period of recuperation at home. His treatment would include prescription drugs and a strict diet, along with limited exercise. As his progress was evaluated, further recommendations would be made.

We assured the doctor of our cooperation and decided to enter the room in small groups, rather than all together. Bruce was alert, but while he acknowledged his mother's presence, I could see him looking for Kevin, waiting just beyond the door.

As Bruce and I reviewed together Dr. Bruno's gratifying

words, I sensed that we were being given a new begin-ning. Our lives would never again be the same. In some ways, I felt closer to him than I had just a few days before. The thought of nearly having lost him made each moment together more meaningful. My single-minded passion was to help him recover.

It turned out not to be an easy task, but at that moment, one for which I was most grateful.

Outside the room, the others were waiting to see their father and rejoice with him in the doctor's encouraging news. We each knew that his main concern was the fact that he would miss Kevin's wedding on Saturday. As the children joined us around the bedside, I could see Bruce's eyes fasten on Kevin. Avoid stress? The unavoidable topic of his absence from the wedding was about to be raised.

Somehow Kevin acknowledged his father's disappoint-ment and adroitly turned the topic into a point of humor. I could feel the tension in the room diminish. First mission accomplished.

A few minutes later, Sally Roberts, Bruce's nurse, ush-ered in our rector, Canon Paul Wancura, and ordered all but two of us to leave during his pastoral call. Bruce's mother and I chose to stay for the celebration of Holy Communion.

In that communion service and our rector's anointing Bruce, I found what I had been seeking. Love and support from family, yes; companionship and compassion from friends, yes; sound and encouraging medical opinion, cer-tainly; prayers and the Scriptures, of course, for which I was most grateful! But added to those, these sacramental acts and our participation in them together helped solidify my faith that God really was in control of our situation.

"O God," our rector prayed, "the strength of the weak

and the comfort of sufferers: Mercifully accept our prayers, and grant to Your servant Bruce the help of Your power, that his sickness may be turned into health, and our sorrow into joy; through Jesus Christ our Lord. Amen.

"Let us bless the Lord."

"Thanks be to God," we responded.

And in my heart, I echoed, *Thanks be to God*.

In the waiting room outside, Ellyn had lingered while her brothers and Belinda had gone on back to Stony Brook.

"We have a lot to praise God for, Mom," she said.

"Indeed, we do, darling," I hugged her and recalled another hospital almost twenty-two years earlier.

Our sons, Don and Kevin, were barely two years and ten months old, respectively, when I announced my third pregnancy. Through all those nine months, I prayed for a daughter. Two little boys were more than sufficient to tax my energies and my patience. In addition, my equally young husband hardly noticed the strain I felt.

We were living on the campus of The Stony Brook School, a college-preparatory boarding school, in a duplex apartment at one end of a boys' dormitory. Our apartment consisted of a kitchen and living room downstairs, two bedrooms and bath upstairs. We lived literally surrounded on the ground floor, second floor, and overhead on the third floor by fifty teenagers, twelfth graders full of energy and pranks. At that time, Bruce was still a junior member of the English department, teaching ninth and tenth graders. But he had taught many of the boys we lived among two or three years earlier, and some of them sang in the chapel choir, which he conducted; others knew him as a runner who sometimes trained with the track team.

In the spring and early summer of 1960, Bruce had made

his second unsuccessful attempt to make the Olympic team. After winning a national championship during the 1960 winter indoor season, his running had pretty much fizzled, and he was no longer a realistic contender. He found this hard to accept, and it made living with him more than trying at times.

Finances were always in short supply, and the prospects of adding another mouth to feed, another pair of shoes to buy, another set of doctor's visits to pay for, also troubled him, I'm sure. Two years earlier, Bruce's promised summer income had evaporated when his employer closed the business; so he had taken up writing as a means of supporting our family over the summer. I can't say that I was impressed by his income potential, since writing articles for educational or religious publications fell somewhat short of the grand scale paid to popular novelists.

Another teacher, Bruce Dodd, with his wife, Carolyn, and two young sons—almost identical in age to ours—lived in a similar apartment at the other end of our dormitory. Our two families were like one family in two separate quarters. Carolyn was my first adult "best friend," someone who understood without having to be told what my life was like because hers was almost the exact mirror image of mine.

The Dodds and Lockerbies did everything together. We were in and out of each other's apartment constantly; we talked late into the night; and when we could afford to hire a baby-sitter, we'd go out for a late-night snack. Sometimes we'd plan one of the mandatory fire drills for our dormitory residents to coincide with our after-midnight return from a local outing. Our husbands would ring the fire alarm, while Carolyn and I sat in the gloom of the dorm lounge and, convulsed with laughter, watched the fifty bleary-eyed and semiclothed sleepwalkers stumble from their rooms and out into the night.

Furthermore, with four little boys between us, we had enough dirty clothes to star in a detergent commercial. So we divided our purchases of laundry necessities, the Lockerbies buying a washer while the Dodds bought the dryer we shared.

Carolyn Dodd had no formal medical training, but she was as close to being a homeopathic physician as anyone I've known. She was an early advocate of health food, introducing me to Adele Davis and "tiger's milk," informing me on ways to supplement the starchy diet we all partook of in the school's dining hall, helping me to cope with the never-ending wash and dirty diapers that were our constant reminders of the joys of motherhood.

For our second pregnancy and delivery, both Carolyn and I had been under the care of an obstetrician in Huntington, New York, about twenty miles from Stony Brook. He'd been recommended by another friend, and, since in those days there were very few obstetricians in our immediate area, we made the journey for our monthly checkups together. No hardship at all because this break in our routine always included lunch and window-shopping.

Kevin had been born at Huntington Hospital. But, to my distress, labor had been a prolonged affair of nearly sixteen hours. When our third child was expected, I vowed that I would never go to the hospital that early again.

On Sunday morning, October 9, 1960, I awoke with the earliest signs that labor was beginning. *Well, not to worry or rush*, I told myself. *I have plenty of time; besides, we now know a shortcut to the hospital, which will cut a few minutes off the trip.*

To give him credit, my husband hovered around me like

a mother hen, insisting that we at least alert the doctor to the situation. I agreed to that, but remained adamant that I wouldn't need to leave home for another few hours. Bruce let me have my way and obediently took the boys with him to his chapel choir rehearsal, assuring me that he'd check on me in about forty-five minutes.

Almost as soon as he was out the door, I felt the first strong contractions. By the time he returned, they had progressed a little in severity, but I felt that I was still in an early stage. I'm not sure just what happened next, but suddenly labor pains made a monumental leap to Stage III, and I knew that, like it or not, this baby was on its way. I realized how far away Huntington Hospital really was! Making it there was now out of the question.

When I relayed this information to the child's father, he looked as though he'd just been knocked down by Muhammad Ali.

"Call the Dodds," was my next command, "and tell them we need help."

"We certainly do!" he shouted back as he ran from our apartment.

I'm sure Bruce really thought I had lost my mind.

Carolyn and Bruce Dodd arrived in our bedroom within seconds.

Bruce Dodd had been a phys ed major and had first-aid training. He was also as levelheaded and caring as any man I knew. If I couldn't have my doctor, Bruce Dodd would certainly do.

Bruce Lockerbie—"my Bruce," as Carolyn or I designated our respective husbands—was sent to locate the school nurse and, if possible, the school's attending physician. My Bruce also made a second call to our obstetrician in Huntington, at this point mainly for moral support.

I could just imagine his opinion of this developing and unnecessarily dramatic medical vignette.

"Whatever you do, try your best not to have the baby delivered in the backseat of a car," the doctor warned. "Can you stay where you are? Is there anyone there to help you?" Bruce assured him that help was at hand.

"I'll see you at the hospital. Good luck."

To my amazement, shortly thereafter, in our apartment bedroom in a boys' dormitory, a baby was born and, to the great relief of my volunteer attendants, without complications. Carolyn had taken immediate control and never for one moment did I doubt her competence. I'll never forget Carolyn holding my seven-pound, thirteen-ounce baby girl for me to see and saying, "Oh, Lory, she's beautiful, and she has dimples!" We named her Ellyn Beth.

My Bruce reappeared shortly after the big event, looking a bit haggard—poor thing!—but with the school nurse and doctor in tow. I was laughing with relief and, at this point, thought them unnecessary; but I finally acquiesced to the medical team's insistence that both mother and baby daughter be sent by ambulance to Huntington Hospital.

The local volunteer fire department's ambulance arrived on this rustic scene, and within a short time we were taking a bumpy ride to Huntington, where we were admitted, feeling rather proud of ourselves indeed.

But when Ellyn was about one month old, she started to manifest the beginnings of what turned out to be a very severe staphylococcus infection. How she contracted this virulent disease we never knew. Perhaps it was a result of the clean but unsterile conditions of her birth. The fact that she was born out of the hospital automatically meant that she was hygienically suspect and unfit to be housed with the hospital-born breed; upon arrival, she was admitted to the "dirty baby" ward, the term given to the isolation nursery.

Her staph infection manifested itself in the form of pustular lesions, which would come and go. Our physician tried one antibiotic after another. Just when we thought the infection was under control, a new lesion would present itself. We were losing confidence in our doctor and in consternation over the fact that our darling baby girl seemed unable to recover from this systemic infection.

Then, in January 1961, when she was just three months old, a simple cold—contracted from one of her brothers, no doubt—appeared to be getting worse and worse. I realized that the baby was becoming seriously ill. Our doctor confirmed my fears that pneumonia had developed and ordered her hospitalized immediately. We consulted a local pediatrician, Dr. John F. Faigle.

The next several days were the most trying we had ever experienced as young parents. Watching our baby through the clear plastic of the oxygen tent—her tiny body struggling for sufficient breath—it seemed almost inevitable that her breathing would fail, that her life would be snatched from us almost before it had begun.

Of course, we were praying for God's mercy in healing our infant daughter. Family, friends, and colleagues were also praying; but we had no confidence that our prayers would be effectual. We had been reduced to a state of hope against hope, a kind of desperation that resigns itself to God's will instead of joyfully claiming God's will.

Then one evening, Stony Brook's headmaster, Dr. Frank E. Gaebelein, called Bruce to his study in his home on the campus. To me and to most of the young wives of Stony Brook faculty, Dr. Gaebelein was always a forbidding figure, a man of high intellect and artistic gifts—a theologian and concert pianist, a nationally acclaimed educator and Alpine mountaineer—too remote from our world of diapers and Dr. Spock, coffee klatches and soap operas, for us or him to feel at ease in each other's company. I can hardly remember ever having had a conversation of more than two sentences with this man whom my husband so admired, respected, and—yes—feared.

When Bruce returned from the headmaster's study, he told me what had happened. Frank Gaebelein was known to be a man of prayer, reputed to pray daily by name for every boy in the school. From the two worn spots on the carpet before his leather sofa and the shiny spots on the sofa cushion, Bruce could see evidence of long hours spent kneeling at that altar.

Dr. Gaebelein said to Bruce, "My wife and I have been praying for your baby. Now I want to show you something very personal and very private."

He reached for two sets of three-by-five-inch cards, held by rubber bands, one marked "Prayer Requests," the other, "Thanksgiving for Answered Prayers."

"I often write prayers as reminders for particular needs. When God has graciously fulfilled my request, I move that prayer card from this pile to that. I keep that answered prayer as a means of thanksgiving."

Then, looking at Bruce with those piercing eyes, Frank Gaebelein said, "I want you to know, Bruce, that today I've moved your daughter's name from my requests to my prayers of thanks."

I was profoundly moved by the faith of this man of God and clung, hoping, to each word, as my husband repeated the story.

It seemed like a miracle to us as, minutes later, our phone rang. The doctor spoke words of encouragement, assuring us that Ellyn had survived the crisis and that her breathing was improving, her temperature returning to normal.

I needed that kind of assurance now. I could put on a convincing act for Bruce and the family, indicating my belief that all would be fine, that we would survive this crisis; but underneath, I wasn't all that confident. I knew I needed to trust the Lord, but not just to come crying to Him as a little girl who was frightened; I wanted to assert the maturity of my years and ask His strength in assuming the responsibilities before me. I needed the knowledge that my Heavenly Father was going through this with me, that I didn't need to face the unknown alone.

This would take, I realized, more than the support of family and friends. Even now, I'm reminded that it's so easy to cruise along, day after day, keeping the faith within the context of our busy lives, giving God a sentence of thanks now and then for all the good things He gives us. Worshiping devoutly on Sunday all too readily becomes part of our routine, but somehow, our faith becomes urgent only when we're in trouble.

I knew that my confidence would only be restored through the reading of Scripture. Over the years, I had experienced this in other situations. Why wasn't I turning to God's Word for direction and encouragement now? Instead of opening my Bible to a favorite passage, I suddenly felt compelled to go to our piano and leaf through the hymn book. I don't play the piano often, but sometimes when I'm sure that I'm alone, I'll sit down and play a few hymns for relaxation. Wondering what I would play at this particular moment, I simply opened the Episcopal *Hymnal* randomly to #662. As my eyes fell on the page,

Take Heart

the words of Henry Francis Lyte's familiar text spoke to
me for the very first time:

> Abide with me: fast falls the eventide;
> The darkness deepens; Lord, with me abide;
> When other helpers fail and comforts flee,
> Help of the helpless, O abide with me.

8
A Necessary Rest

By Monday afternoon, my second full day in cardiac care, I'd begun to rally my spirits sufficiently to give signs of becoming an obstreperous patient. I had no intentions of jumping out of bed and resuming training, but I saw no reason why the mail couldn't be brought in and other business attended to. For instance, it was now June 14, time to address the midmonth bills. Plus, there were all the final details of our side of the wedding to settle. I wanted Lory to bring my Bible and some other reading matter. Furthermore, I wanted access to a phone. Every hospital patient I ever visited had a phone.

"Not my patients in CCU," Sally Roberts told me, and I gathered from her tone that I was no exception. "No, sir, no phones in CCU.

"Besides, Bruce," she went on, "who are you going to call? Your stockbroker? Your bookie? Your girl friend?

Seems to me you've got everything you need coming right here, morning, afternoon, and evening."

Sally Roberts did permit telephone messages to be relayed from the CCU desk, as friends called to inquire about my current state. Visitors were still restricted to family and clergy—although our headmaster, Karl Soderstrom, had been given special allowance—so others had resorted to calling the hospital. To my astonishment, phone calls were coming in from far and near. How could so many people learn so soon of someone's illness? How could so many people care?

"At least let me read yesterday's paper, Sally," I pleaded. That copy of the Sunday *Times* I had purchased en route to the emergency room had somehow been included with my other belongings and placed with them in my bedside locker.

"Okay, but only one section at a time, then you rest. And, only good news," she added. "Dr. Bruno won't allow you to read anything that brings on stress. If I see your monitor jumping, I'll know you're reading bad news!"

I remained in the cardiac care unit and under Sally Roberts's scrutiny until Friday morning. The more I saw of Sally, the more I appreciated her tender toughness, her street-smart way of making a point without losing her commitment to caring. I began to think of her as a coach who keeps on pushing an athlete, in spite of mild or not-so-mild resistance. Like any good coach, she was going to get the best out of those in her charge, whether they liked her or not.

Yet I couldn't not like her—bouncy, peppy, enthusiastic, encouraging. And, as days went by, I began to sense something more about Sally Roberts. I was convinced that she was a born-again believer. I hadn't seen her carrying a Bible or heard her humming hymns; but by her attitude, her bearing, I thought she might be a professing Christian. One morning, I tried my theory.

"Sally, you're a believer in Jesus Christ, aren't you?"

"Yes, I sure am! I'm not allowed to talk about religion to my patients, so I haven't brought it up. But I'm a Christian, and you are too. Know how I know?"

"You were here when my rector came to celebrate Holy Communion."

"True, but that's not why. Lots of folks, when they think they're dying, call for the preacher."

"Maybe you've seen me offer a prayer before I eat?"

"I noticed, but that's not it either."

"What then?"

"I've seen you on television, on 'The 700 Club' couple of times, right? Talking about schools and the Christian family? Connie the cleaning girl's seen you too. In fact, it was Connie who recognized you first.

"Imagine"—she did a Betty Boop imitation—"a *gen-u-ine* TV star!"

I was flabbergasted. As part of promoting two books published by Doubleday in 1980 and 1981, *Who Educates Your Child?* and *Fatherlove*, I'd made the circuit of broadcast interview opportunities, including Pat Robertson's television variety show. But I hadn't considered myself a television star. My only claim to fame was that I managed to make it on and off the set of "The PTL Club" without being hugged by Tammy Faye Bakker! Otherwise, I felt as though my appearances were sort of lost in the shuffle. On one of my "700 Club" visits, my interview had been sandwiched between a Cuban revolutionary and a recipe for granola; the other time, I followed a converted hooker and a faith healer who could make cancerous tumors drop off the body. By comparison, my books, about bringing up and educating children, were rather tame.

Slowly, I began to realize that I was missing the point here. Being on television wasn't what mattered; however, claiming to be a follower of Jesus Christ mattered a very great deal indeed. It wasn't half as important to Sally and Connie whether I had been on TV but whether or not I acted in a manner consistent with my publicly professed faith. In the hospital, in the stress of this intensive care ward, these women could see if a person's religious convictions could carry the weight of whatever known and unknown problems had brought him here. In their own private way, these two relatively new believers—as I later learned—were still watching to see if claims of Christian belief were authentic.

Is there any better crucible than a hospital to test the validity of the Christian faith under real life-and-death conditions? As visitors and, especially, as patients, we're all under the microscope all the time, having our faith observed and evaluated.

Three contrasting examples came to mind. Some years earlier, I had read a novel by D. Keith Mano called *Bishop's Progress*. Its plot revolves around the sudden hospitalization of a fictitious Episcopal bishop of the Diocese of New York—an imagined successor to James Pike and Paul Moore—a churchman whose faith is weighed on the scales and found wanting. In the novel, as I recall, the bishop discovers that his faith is little more than a set of conventional attitudes and social formulas.

At the time I read Mano's novel, I'd had no comparable experience—either as patient or visitor—on which to draw. Apart from an overnight stay for a childhood tonsillectomy, I'd spent no hospital time myself. Like Mano's bishop, I knew nothing at firsthand of the humiliation possible in having one's own clothes taken away and replaced by an embarrassingly skimpy gown; nothing of the leveling effect that being called by one's first name—by young nurses and old orderlies and second-year medical students, not to mention most doctors—has upon self-esteem; nothing of the loneliness the patient feels as the last visitor leaves and the long night begins.

On my occasional hospital visits to see a friend or, rarely, a family member, I must have seemed as wholly unsympathetic to the fears and passions of the sick as any healthy, athletic, and self-centered man in his prime might be. I'm not proud of this fact; I'm simply admitting that I did my best to avoid the obligation of making hospital calls. Perhaps the reason wasn't so much because I was callous toward the plight of the sick as it was that, just being in a hospital worried me, troubled me, frightened me.

In contrast to the bishop in the novel, Richard B. Wollam showed me a better way. A Long Island realtor and insurance broker, Dick Wollam was also among the leaders in giving of himself to our community, serving on boards of various nonprofit agencies. I had first come to know him as the father of two sons attending The Stony Brook School; later, he invited me to join the board of our community library, the Emma S. Clark Memorial Library, of which he was board president.

There I saw him working tirelessly for our community. In spite of enduring the caprices of public apathy and public frenzy over board decisions, Dick Wollam retained a calm and sanguine attitude toward his community service. In the privacy of their home, his wife, Dolores, may have heard Dick express his chagrin over the impossible task facing every voluntary public servant. But with us, whether meeting with us as fellow trustees or sharing a round of golf, he was never so ungracious as to assail the same public he sought so unselfishly to serve.

On my third day in the CCU, I received on my food tray a handwritten letter on yellow legal-size paper. It was from Dick Wollam—to my surprise, a fellow patient in a room just across the hall. He'd been brought in because of recurring chest pains, but he expected to be released soon, as his good-humored note suggested:

> I am only here to help augment the local medical economy till they can find a sick man to replace me:

Then he assured me of his prayers on my behalf.

A postscript informed me that, lacking any writing implement, he had merely sharpened the tip of one of the inedible stalks of asparagus we'd been served for dinner that evening.

Neither of us was permitted out of bed to visit anyone else in the cardiac ward; as expected, he was released the next day, and so I didn't see Dick Wollam until my own recuperation at home was well assured. But his encouragement remained with me. Such was his wit, his personal warmth of concern, his balance between a quiet Christian faith and a humble heart for the good of others.

Nine months later, the warning signs of chest pain returned as a fully charged heart attack; while undergoing bypass surgery, he was further disabled by a stroke. For almost two years, Dick's life held only a mere sliver of its former fullness. Then, amazingly, he made a full recovery, returning to his work and his voluntary service. Together with another local resident, he founded a chapter of the "Zipper Club" for heart surgery survivors to encourage those facing cardiac surgery.

But again he was hospitalized, this time with cancer that ravaged him and took his life in the winter of 1988. On the occasion of his memorial service, the Stony Brook Community Church could not contain the numbers of friends and admirers wishing to attend; the crowd literally overflowed into the street.

I visited Dick Wollam during both his latter hospital stays and found a new joy in making such calls. For no matter his own condition, he always sent me away from his bedside feeling better than when I'd first arrived. Dick had a remarkable capacity for giving encouragement to others, a gift he shared unsparingly.

The third example was my own wife.

Since the early 1970s, Lory had been receiving reports from her doctor that certain cellular changes were being noted in her gynecological tests. "A precancerous condition," it was called; nothing currently major, but worthy of keeping under close and careful watch, especially with a history of cancer in her family. She faithfully scheduled semiannual checkups. Her lab reports generally came back within three weeks, reading "Unchanged."

In the late spring of 1981, Lory realized that the lab report from her last checkup seemed delayed in arriving. She made a mental note to look into the matter, but the call kept slipping from her mind. One day in May, she received a message over her classroom intercom, summoning her to the main office for an important phone call. Leaving her class, she walked through the long corridors of her elementary school, knowing that the call must be significant; otherwise, the school secretary would have taken the message and left a note in her mailbox.

The telephone at the office's reception counter was off the hook and waiting for her.

"This is Lory Lockerbie."

"Mrs. Lockerbie, the doctor would like to speak with you."

In a chilling instant she knew.

"Mrs. Lockerbie? Let me get right to the point of my call. Your most recent lab report shows a dramatic increase in cell dysplasia that we believe needs immediate attention. Can you come to the office this afternoon?"

A busy suburban practitioner, this doctor never had immediate openings in his appointment book. Lory knew that he was stressing the urgency of her condition.

"Is this the first you've known about my report?" Lory asked.

"No," the doctor replied honestly. "It appears that your lab report had been misplaced in our office. I'm very sorry. That's why I'd like to lose no further time in treating you."

Lory put down the phone in shock. Her worst fear, long suppressed by a cheerful disposition, had been that her father's cancer would put her at high risk for the same disease. Now the problem had caught up with her.

And the worst part was, a doctor's office had bungled, not notifying her for weeks!

At that moment, Olga Carlin, the school principal, entered the office. Catching sight of Lory, she recognized the distress of another woman and invited Lory into her office.

When she heard the story, this compassionate woman

said, "It would be wise to have a second opinion. My brother-in-law is one of New York's best OB-GYN doctors. Let me call him and have him see you right away."

Within a day or two, Lory obtained an appointment with Dr. Frederick Silverman, a distinguished Manhattan specialist. He repeated tests and confirmed the diagnosis. Surgery was indicated and a date set for Lory to be admitted to the Women's Pavilion of New York Hospital to undergo a hysterectomy.

Throughout her ordeal—the brief waiting period prior to surgery, the hospitalization itself, her recuperation over that summer of 1981—Lory had demonstrated to me and others a serenity that seemed remarkable to all who saw her—family, friends, colleagues. Beyond her initial distress, she never conveyed anger, only the normal concern that surgery would indeed remove the abnormal cells that were invading the uterus. She never used her situation to manipulate me or gain her own will. In the hospital itself, her nurses told me, she was a cheerful patient, an inspiration to them and to others. Upon returning home, she seemed to draw strength from her weeks of quiet reading, prayer, and meditation, while her body healed.

Faithful in her six-month follow-up appointments with Dr. Silverman, regular also in having mammograms to check for any evidence of breast cancer, Lory has added regular aerobic exercises, brisk walking, and an occasional round of golf to her regimen of healthy cooking and eating. The results are obvious: a beautiful woman of middle years whom no one can believe is a grandmother, a woman whose husband and children respect and cherish her.

Yet, Lory herself would tell you, her near miss with cancer and the surgery that eliminated it were themselves means of grace and avenues to new discoveries about the providence of God, about our need to draw back regularly from the pell-mell pace of life to contemplate its purpose and direction. For if we neglect to take a break voluntarily, we may find ourselves—like it or not—on the disabled list, rendered *hors de combat*, against our will.

Why is it that most of our wisest moments are retrospective, Monday-morning quarterback assessments? Why is our perspective so much more accurate through a rearview mirror?

Looking back, I can now see that God knew just what He was doing, knew just what I needed and when I needed it. True, from my limited vantage, the timing was all wrong. Or was it? Is God's chronometer ever off by so much as a tick? My disability, coming as it did in the summer of 1982, came not a moment too soon to spare me from probable total destruction.

The trouble is, I thought I had already learned this lesson about God's providential care. Not just once or twice, but over and over again. Why didn't the lesson stick? Why did I have to keep being reminded that I'm not in charge of the universe, that God most certainly is?

For instance, nine years earlier, I had learned that sometimes you can see better with one eye than with two. A hemorrhage had blinded my left eye. For several weeks I worried and fretted about my faulty vision, until one evening in Providence, Rhode Island, I learned for the first time the meaning of that word, *providence*. I might have hoped I had learned once and for all that the God whom Abraham knew as *Jehovah-jireh*, the God-who-provides, is also the God who's never caught off base, never off guard, never unprepared, never at a loss. He isn't the God of *accidents*; He's the God of *providence*.

I had once read an interview with the Nobel Prize–winning novelist, Isaac Bashevis Singer, published in the *New York Times*, in which Singer spoke a profound truth:

> In my belief in God, there's only one thing which is steady: I never say the universe was an accident. The word "accident" should be erased from the dictionary. It has little meaning in everyday life and no meaning in philosophy.

For any person who accepts as true the biblical portrait of God as Creator and Sustainer of Life—and especially for the believer who looks to Jesus Christ as Lord of the universe, to whom every element of life is subject—there can be no random event, no unlucky happenstance, no misfortune, no chance meeting nor coincidence, only *providence*.

This may not mean that every microsecond of our lives is divinely planned and programmed for us; that teaching would eliminate the very freedom God grants us to choose wisely or foolishly. But providence does mean that every event of our lives is *provided for:* Our wise choices are provided for, our foolish decisions are provided for; even those incidents in which we're merely secondary players are also provided for. God's grace is that provision, even though sometimes His grace hurts.

It seems that some of us are slower learners than others; so that grace is doubly necessary precisely because the lessons of utter dependence upon God are so necessary to learn and keep on learning. Just as the New Testament says about *chastening*—the archaic word for discipline or rigorous admonition—it's never pleasant to be on either end of the willow switch just inside the woodshed door. Whether you're the parent administering punishment or the child receiving it, chastening hurts. Today, of course, many people are rightly worried about the excesses of corporal punishment, leading to child abuse. Well, while some chastening may go too far in extreme cases, neglect of a child's discipline is always child abuse; but loving discipline is always a sign of parental caring.

Which is why God chastens us—slows us down, if necessary whups us up 'longside our heads, places us flat on our backs, removes from us any semblance of independence or stubborn self-reliance, teaches us one more time to trust and obey, and reminds us what it means to harvest "the peaceable fruit of righteousness" that comes as a result of our chastening (Hebrews 12:5–11).

In time, my sight was restored. Prayer and skillful medical treatment by Dr. George Goodman and his colleague, Dr. Charles Beyrer, then laser surgery by the late Dr. Arnold Breakey, gave me full restoration of my vision. But even if I had remained sightless in that eye—or in both eyes—God's providence would have reigned.

Lying in a hospital's intensive care unit, why couldn't I recall that lesson?

Eventually I learned to submit, but not without a struggle. To a large extent, I was helped by the comfort of the Scriptures and the counsel of friends. One morning, the mail brought a card from Mary and Si Simmons, then colleagues on the Stony Brook faculty. It carried the text of Psalm 116, verses 3 and 4, then 7 and 8:

> The sorrows of death compassed me, and the pains of hell gat hold upon me: I found trouble and sorrow.

Then called I upon the name of the Lord; O Lord, I beseech thee, deliver my soul. . . . Return unto thy rest, O my soul; for the Lord hath dealt bountifully with thee. For thou hast delivered my soul from death, mine eyes from tears, and my feet from falling.

That seemed to be the theme: *rest*. To be sure, enforced rest in a cardiac ward was what the Great Provider had provided for me. A day later, a letter came from Frank Gaebelein, with whom I'd talked about death just a few days before. Now he quoted to me a remarkable passage from John Ruskin:

There is no music in a rest, but there is the making of music in it. In our whole life melody, the music is broken off here and there by "rests," and we foolishly think we have come to the end of time. God sends a time of forced leisure—sickness, disappointed plans, frustrated efforts—and makes a sudden pause in the choral hymn of our lives, and we lament that our voices must be silent, and our part missing in the music which ever goes up to the ear of the Creator. . . .

Then came Ruskin's clincher:

Not without design does God write the music of our lives. But be it ours to learn the time and not be dismayed at the "rests." They are not to be slurred over, not to be omitted, nor to destroy the melody, nor to change the keynote. If we look up, God Himself will beat the time for us. With the eye on Him, we shall strike the next note full and clear.

*　　*　　*

The hardest moments in the process toward submission came when, first Kevin, then Lory, left for the wedding. Father and son had a private moment together; then he was gone to his new role as husband. The next day, it was Lory's turn to leave.

No sooner had she gone than the hospital volunteer brought in the day's mail. A note from Dick Wittman, a friend, a former racing opponent when we were both younger, a sometime training partner, sent me this encouragement just when I needed it most:

> Saturday won't be perfect, but count the blessings. Another wonderful person will become part of the family. Three hundred miles cannot separate the Lockerbie family. You are together. My thoughts and prayers are with you. The best is yet to come.

The best is yet to come! How prophetic he was!

On Friday, the day before the wedding, I was moved out of the confines of cardiac intensive care to the relative freedom of a normal semiprivate room. What a joy to be wheeled through a glass-enclosed overpass connecting two wings of the hospital, to look out and, for the first time in almost a week, see the sunlight. The change of care meant that I was making sure progress toward recovery, that I could now sit up in bed or in a nearby chair, even take an occasional walk in the corridor, while hooked to a Holter monitor that recorded my heart's reaction.

It also meant that I could watch television, make and receive telephone calls, and entertain a few visitors beyond family. I'd been told that a team of friends would be on hand to keep me busy during the wedding celebrations. On Friday evening, during the rehearsal dinner, the first of my supporters arrived: Marvin Goldberg, my long-time friend at Stony Brook who had coached both our sons. He brought with him a stack of books for me to browse or read, plus more than fifty uproarious cartoons about the sport we both love. We laughed throughout his visit, which was interrupted from time to time by a phone call direct from the hotel banquet room in Maryland, where our party was in full swing. It was almost as good a being there in person.

Marvin left me with his assurance that he and his wife, Dorothie, would be at Kennedy Airport—some fifty miles away—the following night to pick up Lory, returning from the wedding reception, and deliver her to my room with a firsthand report on the wedding.

No one could have had a more loyal friend.

Saturday, June 19, was the wedding day. Throughout the afternoon, Bruce Dodd stayed with me. Our friendship went back twenty-five years, to the time when we had been neighbors in the same dormitory, our apartments at opposite ends of the building. Bruce and his wife, Carolyn, had delivered our daughter, Ellyn; their son Scott was an usher in Kevin and Kim's wedding.

For dinner, I discovered a surprise: a glass of wine, prescribed by Dr. Bruno, to celebrate.

At 9:00 P.M., I received a phone call. A female voice said, "Hi, Dad." It was the newest member of our family calling from their honeymoon hotel. "Congratulations, Mrs. Lockerbie," I replied.

An hour later, Lory arrived. We'd worked out an arrangement through Dr. Bruno to allow her to visit after hours. She looked dazzling in her "mother-of-the-groom" dress, and she was full of all those details I wanted to hear. A set of Polaroid photos she brought gave me as good as what the TV networks call "same-day coverage," fully conveying the spirit of the wedding. She also had a cassette tape of the ceremony, including a new song written for the occasion.

Dick Wittman had been right: We'd been together, in spite of the miles.

9
Our Timeless Love

Somehow, as the mother of the groom, I made it through the wedding.

As soon as Kevin had learned of his father's illness—even before he left Chapel Hill to make his detour to the hospital—he and Kim had discussed postponing their wedding date from Saturday, June 19. But Bruce had been adamant that the wedding must go on as planned.

I remember Bruce's speaking to Kevin in the CCU, expressing his disappointment but insisting that, now especially, with the cardiologist talking *recovery*, the wedding should be a joyous occasion. That was the way he wanted it; that was the way it would be.

But all this meant a greater burden on me. On the one hand, yes, relief; but at the same time, my emotions seemed to be riding a roller coaster. Until the heart attack, I had relied on my husband, for the most part, to manage all our household's financial details. I knew I wasn't stupid. I had reared our children, finished an undergraduate degree in anthropology at the State University of New York at Stony Brook, then a master's degree in liberal studies with an emphasis in health education, all the while holding a full-time teaching position in our local public school district. I'd been proud to feel that I was perfectly able to balance the demands of a family and career with some modest success.

However, Bruce was always the organizer *par excellence*, conducting our domestic concerns from all angles, including our family's finances. I guess I just resigned myself to letting him do this. Of course, I had my own checking account, which I managed like a piggy bank, calling for help every now and then when my numbers disagreed with the monthly bank statement.

Not that I wasn't interested in having a more active say in our financial dealings. For years, I had been asking Bruce to include me more in his business decisions and in our family's financial obligations. He preferred to deal with these matters on his own, responding to my questions by pointing to the file cabinet that housed folders marked "Contracts" or "Documents" or "Investments" or "Retirement Plan" and suggesting that I browse through the files. As for our paying bills together, to Bruce it was an inefficient way to operate. He felt that he could whip through a stack of monthly bills by himself far faster than if both of us worked on the task, with his explaining every payment to me.

In that respect, he was probably right. Every so often, we would work together and do the month's bills. Our method never varied. We sat at the kitchen table, the FM radio playing some classical music, with Bruce arranging the pile of envelopes and statements from our various accounts, then filling in the checkbook record and doing the arithmetic, while dictating to me the name of each account and the amount of the check to be written. I would write the check and the return address on the business envelope, then seal the envelope. That was my role in our business partnership. But then we'd miss a month or two, then six, and I would lose track of where the family finances stood.

My terror at suddenly having the responsibility for settling our share of the wedding costs, as well as paying the monthly bills, almost overwhelmed me. I found myself waking up at night, making mental lists of things to do, projecting my worries into the future. How could I have let all those years go by without assuming more responsibility? My conscience must have been wrestling with guilt, and in my typical rebellious nature, I struggled with feelings of anger toward Bruce for having kept me in the dark. How dare he leave me in this unprepared state!

I tried to rationalize my anger by shifting the blame for my inadequacy onto him. Did he need to feel superior? Is that why he had kept me under control? A sexist reaction against his male chauvinism? Maybe, but one that seemed perfectly valid. Or was he simply fulfilling his duty as my husband, taking care of things and sparing me the hassle? In any case, here was the first snag in his plan for our lives.

I resolved that never again would I remain ignorantly in financial La-La-Land.

Waking one night, my mind teeming with anxieties, I remember praying, "Please, God, help me learn quickly what I need to know, and give me the courage to make decisions on my own, without troubling my husband at this critical time."

I soon discovered that my sons were grown men. The boys, as I've always referred to them, were quite capable of assuming control of details relating to the wedding. My list of things-to-do was efficiently being taken care of by our girls—Ellyn and Don's wife, Belinda—who immediately took charge of the day-to-day essentials of our home. Friends came to the house to offer prayer and help in many wonderful ways. Kim, our soon-to-be daughter-in-law, phoned daily, as did her parents. I felt so blessed.

Yet, lurking in my most private thoughts was the nagging fear of widowhood. I could see myself at my husband's funeral service. I knew that in the midst of our wedding plans and festivities, I had come face-to-face with the role of one who mourns.

How strange life is! Rocketing us from one orbit to another, with no time even to fasten the seatbelt!

Somehow the days seemed to pass, as I balanced my hours at the hospital with the increasing demands of the wedding. At the same time, Bruce was beginning to show his concern for what he assumed were details I needed help with.

Wednesday afternoon, almost as soon as I arrived at his bedside, Bruce started in with his organization plan for the rest of the summer.

"Bruno says I'm coming along well enough to be transferred out of CCU by the end of this week."

"That's wonderful, darling," I replied.

"So, that means I'll have a phone and some out-of-bed privileges. I want you to gather up a batch of papers from my study—I'll tell you where they are—and put them in a box, ready to bring in when I get moved."

After a pause, he added, "Do you think they'll let me use a portable typewriter?"

"Are you crazy? I'm not bringing any papers, and you're not doing any business! You're recovering from a heart attack!"

"Mom's right, Dad," Don said. "Lots of time to work, once you get home in a week or two."

"A week or two! I've got a September 1 deadline. There's a hefty check waiting, as soon as the publisher gets that manuscript. We've got bills to pay. I don't have that much time to waste."

"You *won't* have much time," Kevin said ominously, "if you rush into work too soon."

So, we won that battle. Whether or not we would win the war remained to be seen.

A bit subdued, Bruce continued, "I suppose what you're saying also applies to my bookings?"

In July, Bruce was scheduled to speak to the White House Conference on the Family in Washington, D.C., and at two other summer conferences, in addition to several Sunday preaching appointments. His fall and winter had been heavily scheduled—a repeat performance of the past few weeks—as visiting lecturer at the Christian College Consortium's thirteen colleges, along with several other lectureships at seminaries and colleges.

"Will you at least allow me this favor?" Bruce said in a hurt tone. "Please get in touch with Ruth Smith and ask her to draft a letter to the several places I'm supposed to go in the next few weeks to let them know what's happened and tell them that I may have to cancel or postpone—"

"*Will* have to cancel or postpone," I said, revising his dictation.

125

"We'll see what the doctor says," Bruce insisted.

Just before that visit ended, our children left us alone for a few minutes. I could tell that Bruce was troubled about the money. I recalled the doctor's caution about stress, but I knew that repressing what troubles us is even more stressful than getting it talked out.

"I'm worried about insurance, Lory," he said. "Not just the cost of all this"—he indicated the hardware to which he was still attached—"but life insurance. You know how, just a few weeks ago, we were talking about increasing my coverage? Now that'll be almost impossible."

"Don't talk like that," I rebuked him. "We don't need more life insurance. Besides, God knows about those things," I assured him. But in my heart, I too was troubled by any thought of not having the security money brings.

I don't know about your household, but almost every major quarrel we've ever had has been rooted in a money problem. We grew up in quite different economic circumstances: Bruce on the restricted means of a preacher's family; I in a more comfortable environment. Bruce is what I would describe as generous but thrifty, with a decided edge toward *thrifty*. That's especially true when some department store charge account begins to flash the results of a shopping spree. Whenever that happens, I always get brought up short, promptly and unpleasantly. His heritage isn't Scottish for nothing!

At the same time, Bruce is far more willing than I am to take a financial risk. If he could, Bruce would play the stock market; I'd prefer to keep what little money we may have in a certificate of deposit, where I can watch its limited interest accumulate. So sometimes our dispute has been over some investment Bruce wants to explore but which I think is too risky, or some trip Bruce wants to take that I don't think we can afford.

But, more often than not, his ire starts with my shopping, something I've purchased that Bruce doesn't think we need. One of his favorite sayings is, "Lory, you ought to learn the difference between the words *want* and *need.*" We've had some episodes that might have been preludes to World War III and almost always, it seems, over shopping.

All my life I've been a shopper. For me, shopping isn't just buying, it's a recreation. I get more delight out of browsing in a lovely store than I do out of a round of golf. I'm also better at it! I could outlast Grete Waitz in the New York Marathon, if that race were run through Saks Fifth Avenue! I love beautiful things, and okay, I'll admit that all too often I've put more of a strain on the pocketbook than I should have.

We've lived all our life together on the meager stipend paid a boarding-school teacher and administrator, to which Bruce has added his royalties and other earnings. Over the past few years, my salary as a public-school teacher has made possible whatever few luxuries we could afford. Our three children were blessed with sufficient athletic ability for each of them to win a grant-in-aid that covered most of their college bills; otherwise, we would have faced the same mountain of college debt other families encounter. But we too have known what it is to wonder how the next round of bills will be paid. In fact, I doubt that we've ever been free from financial worry.

Looking back, I know that, although we've always managed somehow, my extravagances put pressure on us. Was the Lord now using this experience to teach me to be more aware of my limits?

*   *   *

Friday morning, I awoke with the resolve that nothing should spoil this wonderful occasion for Kim and Kevin. We had planned that, after a brief visit to the hospital, I would fly to Baltimore-Washington Airport, only a few minutes from Columbia, Maryland, to join the celebration and preside at the rehearsal dinner later that evening.

Bruce was in especially good spirits when I arrived, anticipating being moved from CCU to another, less restrictive ward. I'm grateful that, in a special way, he submerged his own disappointment and gave me the support and encouragement I needed to go through it alone.

We also had arranged that two very close friends would sit with him Friday evening and Saturday afternoon, the time when wedding thoughts would be most on his mind. Friends would also pick me up at the airport on Saturday night and deliver me to the hospital for my own version of "Eyewitness News."

So, equipped with a Polaroid camera and tape recorder, I found myself alone on a plane heading for our son's wedding. For one more fleeting moment of doubt, as thoughts and emotions flooded my mind, I dared to ask God the unanswerable question, *"Why?"*

Yet, in spite of my perplexity, the wedding celebration was as perfect as one could hope. To begin, I'd brought with me a tape-recorded greeting Bruce had made to be played at the start of our rehearsal dinner. Just hearing his voice, welcoming everyone to the party he was missing, made me proud to stand up and add my own welcoming words. And with them, I was able, at least, to thank God for sparing my husband's life.

Of course, everyone expressed such kindness. Kim's

pastor, Dr. Daniel Cox, rector of the Bishop Cummins Memorial Church in Catonsville, who would officiate at the marriage ceremony itself, was especially compassionate. Just knowing that so many friends had come from so far away to stand with me gave me an added measure of strength.

Kim was a gorgeous bride. Ellyn and Belinda were among her attendants; Kevin had Don as his best man and his Stony Brook buddies as ushers. Mark Hanchett sang a song, "Our Timeless Love," that Bruce and Werner Janssen had written just for this occasion—as they'd also done for Belinda and Don's wedding two years before. The words and music lifted me above my temporary sadness at being alone.

> *By ring and kiss and prayer we've made our vow*
> *To live each day in love, as we are now.*
> *So take my hand in yours—I give you mine—*
> *From this day forth, to share our love divine;*
> *And through the coming years, our joys, our hopes, our fears,*
> *Will teach the blessings of our timeless love.*

As I listened, I thought of my own wedding, almost twenty-six years earlier.

We had been engaged since February 1956, over ten months, and dating each other exclusively for more than three years—too long, as I now believe—before our wedding day in December finally arrived. I finished nursing studies in late summer, took a job at my hospital, and spent every free moment preparing for the ordeal of New York State's exams to become a registered nurse. During those few months, I lived at home with my mother and brother, while working the evening shift, 4:00 P.M. to midnight, at the hospital. In those days, I commuted fearlessly by subway, even on the return trip home at night. Today, I wouldn't dare ride the same subway at high noon!

Those few months, from September to December, were my first and only experience as a semi-independent adult. I was twenty years old and still living in my mother's house, but I had a nursing diploma, and I hoped soon to add the initials *R.N.* after my name. Meanwhile, I had a responsible job, heading a surgical floor.

But was I ready for marriage? I hardly think so. Neither was Bruce.

We had grown accustomed to each other in a youthful way, never really having had the experience of comparison with others. Young people—especially professing Christians—didn't "live together" before marriage, as seems so customary today. We thought we knew each other so well; yet now, I realize, I knew so little about him—or about myself.

During those very important months before our wedding, Bruce and I were separated. In the spring of 1956, his father had taken a new church in Buffalo, New York. Following his graduation from NYU in June, Bruce had gone to Buffalo to join his family and work in his father's church, while preparing for his Olympic qualifying trials in August.

Unhappily, he contracted a severe virus a few days before the Olympic trials, ran poorly in his race, and missed making the team. His disappointment pained him deeply. I joined him in Buffalo for a week's vacation just before he left for graduate school and a teaching fellowship at Wheaton College, near Chicago. I remember that week as one that was hardly as idyllic as it should have been for a couple about to be married. We were both frustrated over the summer-long separation, and Bruce, near despair at having missed his greatest goal, was particularly moody. Now we faced another three months apart.

Our letters hadn't conveyed all the anxieties we were both feeling about our future together. I've never been that great at letter writing; still, I looked critically at all of Bruce's letters, expecting his constant declarations of undying love. If I didn't feel he was expressing himself as adequately as I hoped, I didn't hesitate to let him know my doubts about our relationship.

Admittedly, at age twenty, I was still very much a child, scarcely ready for the transfer to living with someone still not sure what he wanted to do with his life. The week wasn't at all what I had expected.

When Bruce got to Wheaton, matters didn't greatly improve. Our long-distance arguments were casting a cloud over our engagement. Telephone calls began replacing letters, and as the months between August and December narrowed, our tensions mounted. We were both wondering whether we were making a mistake in marrying at that time. I knew we needed to see each other and make a decision one way or the other.

So, in early November, just six weeks before our scheduled wedding date, I flew to Chicago to settle the fear that seemed to be shadowing us. Did we really love each other more than anything or anyone else? Were we ready to commit ourselves to each other?

That weekend was a turning point. Bruce somehow seemed ready for my anxieties. He met me at the airport looking very handsome indeed; he also seemed more mature. We drove back to Wheaton and talked endlessly about the months that had separated us, about our mutual concerns. Suddenly it was as if we had never been apart. Our joy at being reunited intensified as he showed me the apartment that would soon become our first home. That weekend remains vivid in my memory. We recommitted ourselves to each other, and with that reassurance blotting out any pangs of insecurity, I returned home ready to send out our invitations and make the final preparations for our wedding.

I don't remember much about that wintry day—December 15, 1956—except that I made my vows sincerely, almost utterly ignorant of how far they'd be tested . . .

> I, Lory, take you, Bruce, to be my husband, to have and to hold from this day forward, for better for worse, for richer for poorer, in sickness and in health, to love and to cherish, till death us do part.

As a young girl about to become a married woman, I thought I knew what those words meant. I recited them sincerely at the time; but just saying or hearing those traditional words in no way prepares you for living through the actual situations, as they may arise. As years passed, our marriage included almost all the phases most couples go through. The reality of Bruce's heart attack was as close as I cared to come to the final phrase of our wedding vows.

I believe that the groundwork you lay as the foundation of your marriage gives you the strength necessary to deal with the bad times, along with the good. If you find yourself crumbling under the pressure that comes to us all, at one time or another, it's probably because the marriage commitment hasn't been sufficiently nurtured; the vows haven't taken hold.

We started our life together on a high plane. Life

couldn't be better; we were young and healthy, both working, and we knew we were in love. Quickly, however, the family scene began to change, as our children arrived. At that time, the primary focus of our attention shifted toward them. This is a crucial adjustment for most couples, for it's at that point in the marriage that relationships become strained.

Had there ever been a time when I considered rescinding my vow? I like what I've heard Ruth Bell Graham, wife of Billy Graham, say: "Divorce? Never! Murder? Frequently!" Of course, like anyone else's, our marriage had had its ups and downs. There had been times when I worried about Bruce's love for me, my love for him. There'd been times when I felt that our love was fading. It might have been easy to look in another direction, but the basic belief that we had committed ourselves to each other held firm at the root of our relationship. I further believe that we were both compelled by our sense of mutual responsibility to our children to provide them with stability. To deny our basic beliefs would have been disastrous to us both.

With maturity and the passage of time also comes the growth of various, perhaps as yet unrecognized, facets of our personalities. I began to see my husband in a more tender light. I also realized that I was less competitive with him. We were two different people with differing interests and abilities, as well as some very wonderful traits in common. As I developed into womanhood, I became more comfortable with myself as a person. My own self-esteem improved with the realization that I was accomplishing the goals I had laid out for myself. My attitudes concerning faith, my husband, family, friends, and career all seemed to fall into perspective; we began to share with each other things that mattered most to us both.

Bonding is a popular word today. It means the nurture and development of a significant human relationship, one that causes two persons to adhere together. I think of our marriage in this way: We've been *bonded* by the intensifying of our union. My husband has become my best friend. We share daily with each other, trying never to take each other for granted, but with humor and humility experiencing the full meaning of the words *to love and to cherish*.

On that day so long ago, there had been a wedding song for me too, written by Bruce, its text, the beautiful words from the Song of Solomon,

> *Set me as a seal upon thy heart, for love is strong.*
> *Many waters cannot quench love, neither can the*
>   *floods drown it.*
> *My beloved is mine, and I am his,*
> *Until the day break and the shadows flee away.*

Then Bruce's father closed our wedding ceremony by reminding us that there would come a day, sooner than this afternoon's glow of rapture might predict, when one of us would become angry at the other, when nasty words would fly between us, in spite of love, in spite of all we cherish.

"At times like those," my new father-in-law urged us, "remember the words of Saint Paul to the Ephesians."

> And be ye kind one to another, tenderhearted, forgiving one another, even as God for Christ's sake hath forgiven you.

Words I can never forget. Words that set the seal of timeless love forever.

*   *   *

Did that young couple standing before me in a Maryland church, so dewy-eyed and trembling with sincerity, understand all this any better than my generation? Perhaps so. Will they ever need a near calamity to remind them to love and to cherish each other until death? I hope not.

After the receiving line, I had time only to hug the bride and groom before rushing away from the wedding reception to catch the last plane from Baltimore to Long Island. Friends from Stony Brook, Marvin and Dorothie Goldberg, picked me up at the airport and drove me directly to the hospital. By special permission, long after regular visiting hours, I was admitted to Bruce's room. I sat quietly by his bed, holding his hand. He listened eagerly as I recaptured the events of the last two days the best way I could. We examined photographs and listened to a tape cassette of the wedding ceremony. We both cried a little as we heard the wedding vows, knowing then as never before the real meaning of those words.

Driving home that night—for the first time all week to an empty house—I knew that we had both survived the most difficult week of our lives . . . each of us in a different way. I knew that our lives would be forever changed, and although I couldn't claim to see into the future, I had a very real sense that I was stronger for having had the experience, better prepared for coping with whatever might lie ahead.

I slept all that night without waking.

10

A Divinity
That Shapes
Our Ends

Dr. Bruno released me from the hospital a week later, on Friday, June 25.

Since being transferred from CCU, my progress toward recovery had been on an upward curve. I was walking each day. Walking? Not really; at first, more like shuffling in my slippers. I was stunned by how wobbly I felt, like a clown on stilts. I stayed close to the corridor wall, almost like a ballet dancer holding on to the bar; but over time my hips and legs grew steadier and my balance improved. Lory even bought me a new pair of Nike walking shoes to make my perambulations less ungainly. Putting on those shoes twice a day seemed like preparing for a workout.

I had my walking route laid out. Turning left out of my room, I would head down the corridor to its end, then back to the nursing station in the middle of the hallway; left again into the glass-enclosed overpass between build-

ings for some sunlight and a full view of the world outside; back to the corridor and left once more to its opposite
end, before reversing for the return trip to my room.

My problem was keeping pace and time out of my mind.
Even in just that simple stroll, hardly as much as half a lap
on a high school track, I was already thinking about post-
ing daily records and making note of personal bests. My
old competitive spirit remained unquenched, ready to take
on new challenges, however diminished in scope. Instead
of competing to be among the fastest runners over forty,
I'd settle for winning the hospital corridor snail crawl for
recovering heart attack patients.

In a certain sense, that was a good sign. Foolish as it
seems, my clocking those twice-a-day walks along my
third-floor route suggested something hopeful about my
mental condition. It meant that the brush with death
hadn't eliminated my desire to face life head-on and do
my best to excel. It meant that I hadn't been so utterly
traumatized by my sudden illness that I couldn't do anything but retreat into the security of idleness and wait for
the end to come.

In another respect, however, timing my walks was the
wrong approach to exercise. It meant that my overly competitive nature was still in control; it meant that I hadn't
learned anything at all about the value of a simple, leisurely walk; that I was still too intensely concerned about
getting from *here* to *there* as fast as possible to bother stopping along the way for a conversation or a few moments of
observation. In fact, I can recall being annoyed when, on
those walks, an orderly's cart or some group of visitors to
someone else's room would emerge in the corridor just
ahead of me, either blocking my path or causing me to

swerve—a maneuver my still uncertain limbs had trouble negotiating.

Someone on the nursing staff must have spotted me checking my stopwatch en route. The next time he came to call, Dr. Bruno made it very clear that he wanted the timing business stopped.

"I appreciate your eagerness to get back in the saddle," he told me. "Just leave the watch here in the room. You don't have to push yourself just yet.

"By the way," he added, "we'll be giving you a stress test before you're discharged. We'll put you on a treadmill for a few minutes. You can show your stuff then."

I took the watch off and put it away temporarily. I would have to find something else to challenge me.

Hospitals are like freshman dormitories at boarding school or college: You don't get to choose your roommate or his family and friends who come to visit. You get wheeled into a room, deposited on the bed—somehow the present occupant always seems to have the bed next to the window—and hope, first, that he's not in such mortal pain that his groanings become yours; second, that he's not a closet smoker who sneaks his nicotine fix in the same bathroom you have to use; third, that his relatives are semicivilized enough to stay in their half of the room and leave promptly when visiting hours end.

Most important, you hope that he's not looking to bend your ear all day and night. Illness or injury of any description almost always carries with it the symptoms of another infection: self-absorption. It is one of our most human traits. Whether our malady be a headache or a hangnail, when pain or discomfort strikes, we focus solely on ourselves. We become the center of our own attention, and because pain convinces us that we are the only person who matters, we expect everyone else to concentrate on our concerns. For that reason, most hospitals are full of people sick and dying from the worst disease of all: egocentric affection, self-love to the exclusion of anyone else.

The dominant symptom of this disease is well-known; some humorist has called it "giving an organ recital." The patient has a fixation on talking about his own precarious condition—the gravity of his own morbidity—to anyone within earshot, magnifying his own awful predicament, showing the wound or scar or other physical evidences of suffering endured, accusing all previous medical caregivers of incompetence, making unreasonable demands upon current nurses, blaming current doctors for not telling all they know about his case. All this without much, if any, show of concern for anyone else. Or if someone else should seek to insert a word about his own complaint, the standard response to such an intrusion is what I've grown to recognize as the "That's nothing!" syndrome. No matter how serious your sickness may be, the ultimate one-up-on-you is to say, "That's nothing! You should see *my* X rays!"

The most obvious aspect of self-absorption with one's own ailment is the way we customarily badger any innocent party unhappy enough to be assigned to the same hospital room with us. In that common bond of medical dependency, nothing's sacred, nothing's private. Somehow, the shared circumstances of illness and hospital confinement seem to force upon the unwary our need for self-disclosure, a state the poet Karl Shapiro describes as "like convalescents, intimate and gauche."

Pity the poor soul who gets a garrulous roommate, especially some incessant talker who's been hospitalized long enough to have had two or three preceding room-mates whom he's already wearied to death! The sagas of their demise, added to his own heroic—and, to date, successful—struggles to ward off the Grim Reaper, make for compelling monologues! Or, so he thinks.

By nature, I'm not a particularly talkative person, espe-cially when it comes to striking up a conversation with people I don't know. I can fly for five hours across the continent and not engage the person next to me, unless it seems appropriate. I can sit in a waiting room or at a track meet and not feel any need to accost strangers with my opinions. I can't imagine responding to the conventional question, "How are you?" by reciting my medical history. For the purposes of a book like this, okay; but in general discourse, never.

So, one of my least promising prospects, in leaving the isolation of CCU, was the probability of having a room-mate, maybe a nonstop talker. It never occurred to me that I might benefit from having such a companion, never mind that I might be of some comfort and support to him.

As it turned out, one of my roommates, Peter—the first-names-only policy also prevails among patients—had a lot to talk about and a need for someone to listen. We were together only a couple of days, but in that short time, I came to know his life story and comprehend, if only slightly, the fears he faced.

He had had several attacks before undergoing bypass surgery, replacing narrowings of the arteries in his heart with cleaner vessels taken from the leg. But in Peter's case, the surgery hadn't been wholly successful. He was still suffering acute angina, a condition probably not helped by the fact that he hadn't been able to quit his smoking habit.

Peter represented the ideal of a strong family man, a

loving and faithful husband and father, a good neighbor. But he couldn't resolve the seeming unfairness of life.

"Too many bad things happening to innocent people," he'd say.

"Maybe we're not supposed to understand all God's mysteries," I answered. "Maybe we're just supposed to accept His sovereignty and go on from there."

"No, that's too simple," Peter protested. "I can't buy that. Take you, you're a bright guy, a teacher and all that. Maybe it makes sense to you, getting hit by a heart attack at your age, nice wife and all. Missing your kid's wedding, you tell me, and all."

We talked on, quite civil in our disagreeing over the nature of God. I was conscious of not wanting to belabor a subject on which it seemed Peter had made up his mind. But whenever I fell silent or attempted to redirect the topic, he'd pick it up again with another question of theology, another point of controversy, another brief in his long-running quarrel with God.

"For instance, I see you praying when your food tray's brought in."

I tried joshing with him. "Don't you think we *need* to pray before we touch this stuff?"

Then I offered the suggestion that prayers of thanksgiving and petitions for blessing on our food were really expressions of gratitude for all of God's gifts to us.

"The word *grace* just means 'gift,' " I explained. "That's why some people refer to 'saying the grace before dinner.' It means acknowledging God's grace in providing us with the gifts of life and food.

"Since I've been in this hospital, Peter," I continued, "I've been saying a little prayer of my own every morning and several times a day. Want to hear it?"

141

"Sure."

"I just say, 'Thank you, Lord, for life, for love, for work and the strength to do it, for play and the sense to enjoy it.' "

"That's all?"

"That's all. What else is there?"

"Well, I like that last part, 'play and the sense to enjoy it.' I haven't done much playing in my life. Too busy working. Maybe I needed more time to play. Then I wouldn't be here today."

The next morning, Peter got the bad news he'd most been fearing. His doctor had determined that the only possible relief for his angina would be to open his chest again and repeat the bypass procedure.

What encouragement could I offer?

It was just before noon, and I had decided that this would be the day I'd shave for the first time since arriving at the hospital, eleven days earlier. When I emerged from the tiny bathroom adjoining our room, I found that our food trays had been delivered while I was shaving. Peter was sitting on the edge of his bed, his food as yet untouched.

"I was thinking I'd wait until you—uh—uh—say a prayer with me," he said.

"Sure, Peter," and I offered the prayer that I'd learned from Lory's Roman Catholic childhood:

> Bless us, O Lord, and these Thy gifts which we are about to receive from Thy bounty, through Christ our Lord. Amen.

"That's not the prayer I meant," Peter said. "I know that prayer. I meant the prayer you invented, about work and play."

And so I prayed again,

> Thank you, Lord, for life, for love, for work and the
> strength to do it, for play and the sense to enjoy it.

Then I added, "And bless Peter and make him strong to
face his surgery."

This time, the "Amen" came from my roommate's lips.
When I raised my eyes, he had just completed making the
sign of the Cross.

I spoke to Peter on the day these words were typed,
seven years later. He's had still another bypass, this time
replacing six clogged vessels. We wished each other well.

When I wasn't talking to roommates, I spent my time
reading. Along with the many cards and letters that arrived in each day's mail, some friends had given me a
variety of books—a collection of *New Yorker* cartoons, a
theological treatise on knowing God's will, John Cheever's
short stories, and Norman Cousins's *Anatomy of an Illness*,
describing how a changed diet combined with laughter
and willpower achieved what conventional medical science could not.

Along with these, I was rereading Shakespeare. Our
local Public Broadcasting channel had scheduled a repeat
of its series, "The Shakespeare Plays," with all those mar-
velous British actors. Since college days—and particularly
as an English teacher—I've been a devotee of Shakespear-
ean drama. I remember, as an undergraduate, seeing a
young and not-yet-balding Pernell Roberts play Macbeth,
some years before his TV role as Adam Cartwright in "Bo-
nanza." I remember a weekend at Stratford, Ontario,
when we saw Christopher Plummer, on consecutive

nights, as Sir Andrew Aguecheek in *Twelfth Night* and as Hamlet, and the thrill of seeing Lee J. Cobb in *King Lear* and James Earl Jones in *Othello*.

This PBS series included several plays I had never seen in production. I asked Lory to bring me my copy of Shakespeare's *Collected Works* so that I could read ahead of each broadcast. But instead of limiting myself to just the plays on TV, I read through the entire set of the Bard's dramas. It's amazing how, as with the Bible, reading an enduring work of literature—a classic—never fails to reveal a new insight into the text and its meaning.

I must have read and taught a play like *Hamlet* or *Macbeth* more than a hundred times, line-by-line, scene-by-scene, to different classes. Yet in that hospital room, I came upon a particular speech by Hamlet, as if for the first time, whose meaning spoke to me in new ways.

At the beginning of the play's final scene, Hamlet is explaining to his friend Horatio how he escaped his uncle Claudius's scheme to have pirates assassinate him. He speaks of having had trouble sleeping and how, in that sleeplessness, he'd discovered the plot against him:

> Sir, in my heart there was a kind of fighting
> That would not let me sleep.

Sleep is generally considered to be a blessing; the inability to sleep, a curse. So, in another instance, Macbeth laments his loss of sleep,

> . . . the innocent Sleep,
> Sleep that knits up the ravel'd sleeve of care.

Macbeth rightly fears that, in committing murder, he has murdered Sleep, and therefore,

Macbeth shall sleep no more!

Ever since my first night in the hospital, when three other patients had died in rooms next to me, I had been struggling with insomnia. Sometimes after my last evening visitors had gone, the television or portable radio would be turned off, the lights brought down, and an evening-shift nurse would check my vital signs, replenish my IV drip bags, and administer that day's final dosage of nitro-glycerin paste, nifedipine capsules, and the belly-bruising injection of Heparin, along with a Valium tablet to help me sleep.

Soon thereafter, I would respond to the drug and fade into sleep. But after a couple of hours, I would waken and remain awake until near dawn. In fact, most nights I fell back to sleep just before the morning shift arrived to greet me with the first Heparin punch in my gut. Then I'd doze on and off all morning, reading in snatches until Lory's afternoon visit and the Shakespeare play.

Initially, I supposed that I was reacting to the working noise of the night shift on duty. It's hard for us patients to realize that, while we're supposed to be asleep, it's like nine-to-five out at the nursing station. Between rounds, the night staff talks and laughs and plays the radio; the hospital intercom calls doctors as needed; orderlies and other workers push carts, wash floors, and clatter bed-pans. It's all in a normal tour of duty.

Meanwhile, Mrs. McNulty across the hall was carrying on her incessant and unbalanced diatribe against the world. Hour after hour, unless otherwise incapacitated by calmative drugs, she screamed the same four-sentence refrain:

"Help! They're killing me in here! My son's out to steal

my money! The nurse has got my purse! Help! They're killing me in here! My son's out to steal my money. . . ."

You get the picture? Sleeping through such a caterwauling of necessary industry mixed with the outcries of human tragedy would tax a double dose of Valium. So the prescription was switched to a stronger pill called Halcion. Still I wakened and stayed wide-eyed until the next nurse passing saw my bedside light aglow.

"Still can't sleep, Bruce? What do we have to do, hit you with a brick?"

I began to worry that I too had murdered Sleep. But I knew it wasn't just bad dreams that were waking me; it was a pervading fear of death. I was afraid to deliver myself over into each night's unconsciousness, lest I not survive to see the morning. Even though I'd felt at peace when reciting the Twenty-third Psalm with Lory—even though I claimed to believe that God would deliver me from the fear of the shadow of death—nonetheless that fear obsessed me.

One night, during my insomnia, I was finishing my reading of *Hamlet* and came to the passage already cited. But unlike Macbeth, whose insomniac nights were the result of a blood-stained conscience, Hamlet, it seems, had been the recipient of God's own *providential insomnia*, from which he obtained this lesson:

> There's a divinity that shapes our ends,
> Rough-hew them how we will.

Providential insomnia. Sometimes it affords us a firsthand view of God's role as Divine Designer who makes all the pieces fit, no matter how crudely we strew them about; a Master Planner who resolves all the conflicts; a Carpenter uniquely able to plane and polish the rough edges that we bring for His use.

If an Elizabethan dramatist, speaking as a Viking prince, could believe in such divine care, why couldn't I?

Setting aside my Shakespeare, I began thinking about others who might be said to have had the same sort of experience, the gift of a sleepless night. Certainly, Ahasuerus, sultan of the Medes and Persians, could qualify, according to the account recorded in the Book of Esther (6:1):

> On that night could not the king sleep, and he commanded to bring the book of records of the chronicles; and they were read before the king.

Could anything make for duller listening than the census statistics and police blotter report from the archives of ancient Sushan? Certain to put any king to sleep! But in the middle of a boring passage comes an electrifying story about a conspiracy against this very king, and a man named Mordecai who had revealed the threat but had never been rewarded for his loyalty. In the providence of God, the king's insomnia leads to Mordecai's elevation and, because of him, his cousin Esther, the queen, will be able to deliver the Jews from the evil Haman.

Providential insomnia. Sometimes it reveals the grace of God in deliverance.

I thought also of a passage in Henry David Thoreau's appeal, "On Behalf of Captain John Brown." Archly opposed to slavery, an advocate of abolitionism, and a resister to the infamous poll tax, Thoreau had been much moved by John Brown's daring raid, in 1859, on the arsenal at Harper's Ferry, Virginia, in hopes of freeing the slaves. Brown failed, of course, becoming instead the subject of a folk song, "John Brown's Body Lies A-Moulderin' in the Grave." But his fanaticism inspired Thoreau's own, more moderate but nonetheless historic, civil disobedience. It also led to Thoreau's instance of productive sleeplessness. He wrote,

> I kept a pencil under my pillow, and when I could not sleep, I wrote in the dark.

Providential insomnia. If Thoreau could make effective use of his wakeful nights, so could I. From that time on, I resolved to pray for God's gift of peaceful sleep through deliverance from fear. I prayed also for grace to deal with the absence of sleep, to use it as a time, not merely to count sheep or plan financial strategies, but for rehearsing God's many instances of grace in my life. Finally, if sleep still eluded me, I'd take it as a sign from God to "write in the dark."

The next time I awoke in the middle of the night, I began writing a detailed recapitulation of the previous few days' events. Those notes, preserved since 1982, have served me well in recalling as accurately as possible the story that lies behind this book.

Not, however, with a pencil kept under my pillow; Lory nixed that idea as carrying Thoreau's metaphor to literal extremes. Instead, as an alternative, she showed me a passage in Proverbs 3:24–26:

> When thou liest down, thou shalt not be afraid: yea, thou shalt lie down, and thy sleep shall be sweet. Be not afraid of sudden fear, neither of the desolation of the wicked, when it cometh. For the Lord shall be thy

confidence, and shall keep they foot from being taken.

Following several routine tests, with such exotic names as "gated pool" and"thallium myocardial perfusion imaging," to determine my current status, Dr. Bruno announced that I was fit to go home. During a limited and carefully monitored ten-minute treadmill trek, my heart rate had moved from 71 to only 116; my blood pressure had risen to 130/85, within an acceptable range.

"We're still puzzled over your initial attack," the doctor told me, "and the fact that you had such intermittent warnings. There's some recent research into a phenomenon called *silent ischemia*, which means the kind of cardiac condition that carries with it little or no angina.

"We'll be following your case carefully. I've scheduled a stress test for two weeks from today, and we'll talk more after that. In the meantime, take it easy, avoid stress as much as possible, and watch what you eat. Here are some suggestions for your new diet."

He handed me some photocopied pages of instructions for more healthy eating and controlled exercise.

"Keep in touch, Bruce. You're a lucky man."

"More than lucky, Doctor. Blessed."

"Right, blessed. See you in two weeks."

11
Coping With Life

The summer of 1982 turned out rather differently from the way we'd planned. Bruce arrived home from his hospital stay with a list of do's and don't's that I was determined to enforce. Nurse Ratchett would have nothing on me!

In an attempt to regain my own confidence in my somewhat tarnished nursing reputation, I had taken from the library everything I could read about heart disease; I even dusted off my old medical textbooks for further information. I was obsessed with Bruce's diet. In fact, I was quite sure that I was at least partly to blame for the years I had let slip by, allowing my husband to dictate what he would and wouldn't eat.

But all that would change. Now the words *fat, palm* or *coconut oil, cholesterol, salt, sugar* leaped off the list of ingredients on every package of food I examined in the supermarkets. Being a reader of cookbooks and collector of recipes, I found myself replacing old favorites with those in books such as Francine Prince's *Diet for Life*. Mrs. Prince tells an enlightening story of how, as a nutritionist, she sought to preserve her husband from open heart surgery by radically altering his eating. It seemed to have been a successful treatment and, for them, well worth the time invested in preparing her own substitutes for all the no-no's common to standard American diet.

Much of what I read, however, seemed overwhelming in its intensity and commitment. Something was telling me to attack this problem with a large dose of common sense too. After the first few weeks of learning to cook all over again, I aimed at following a basic diet of chicken, fish, vegetables, fruit, and grains, as suggested by the American Heart Association.

I soon realized that if I simply eliminated processed foods and used only fresh ingredients, I was practically home free. In recent years, we've included oat bran in our diet; every morning at breakfast, we enjoy a homemade muffin. When I first read about the wonders of oat bran in lowering cholesterol, I had to hoard boxes of oat bran flour. Now the miracle ingredient is widely publicized and amply available, so hoarding is no longer necessary.

I felt proud of myself for preparing food as attractively and tastily as I could, omitting the unhealthy ingredients that I used to include. Little by little, I became much more aware of garnishing my dishes with fresh herbs—basil, oregano, dill, for instance—and low-fat ingredients, which can be quite satisfying alternatives to what some recipes call for.

Bruce and I both lost weight—a bonus benefit for me— and we set into a regimen of daily activity suggested by

Dr. Bruno's office. We walked together each day, and Bruce was allowed a brief time for writing and other desk work, but I also enforced an afternoon nap. During this hour or two, I would escape and refresh myself at our local beach club. Just sitting by the water's edge, looking across Long Island Sound to the Connecticut shoreline or reading was wonderfully relaxing, and I'd return to my improving patient in good spirits.

In the late afternoon, we often had visitors drop by to see how Bruce was doing. Our evenings were quiet— reading, listening to music, watching television. I could see my husband's health improving, and just the slower pace of our life together seemed to be therapy in itself.

About six weeks after releasing Bruce from the hospital, Dr. Bruno scheduled him for an angiogram. He explained that this procedure was really the only accurate test to show conclusively the actual state of Bruce's coronary arteries. Only by viewing the X-ray photos of the heart, as the catheter probe inserted into a vessel in the groin snakes its way to the heart itself, could a cardiologist specify which arteries had been narrowed or closed by arteriosclerosis; only in this way could a doctor define how much damage had been done to the heart muscle itself.

In mid-August we went to St. John's Episcopal Hospital in Smithtown, New York, six miles from home, in the opposite direction from Port Jefferson's Mather Hospital. Bruce in particular wasn't overjoyed to reenter the hospital. His father's unpleasant experiences with the angiogram procedure had made a strong impression on him. I remember being moderately apprehensive, but we trusted Peter Bruno's judgment, and we meekly followed his instructions.

Several other acquaintances were encouraging about the

procedure, telling us that there really wasn't anything to worry about. We weren't even depressed by the obligatory visit of the cardiologist on the evening before the angiogram, reminding us of the often-overlooked fact that every surgical procedure carries with it some degree of risk—heart failure, stroke, other complications.

The morning the angiogram was to be performed, I sat in the waiting room, anticipating a postoperative conversation with the doctor. I felt certain—I *knew*—he would have good news. In fact, I rather wondered if this test might not show that the original diagnosis of an acute myocardial infarction had been wrong. After all, Bruce seemed to be recovering so well and had had no pain whatever.

As the time dragged on, however, my bravado changed to increased anxiety. Where was Dr. Bruno and why was it taking so long? After what turned out to be several hours, he was suddenly standing before me, uttering the words, "Well, he certainly gave us a rough time."

Apparently, the initial insertion of the catheter had been difficult. When it was finally in place and the dye that highlights the vessels under X ray had been administered, Bruce's heart went into a spasm of fibrillation, or erratic contractions, so violent that the doctors had to use electrical paddles, called defibrillators, on his chest to resuscitate him. Another close call.

Telling me his report, Dr. Bruno looked as distressed as I felt.

"You mean, we almost lost him again?"

The doctor assured me that Bruce was by then resting comfortably and led me to a staff conference room, where he showed me the films produced by the angiography and interpreted them for me. These films were conclusive in supporting the original diagnosis. I could see how the left descending anterior coronary artery was just about totally blocked. The right artery also showed blockage but somewhat less. Considerable damage had been done to the lining, where the lack of blood had led to an insufficient supply of oxygen. Yet the doctor believed that, in time, healing could take place through what he called "collateral circulation," meaning that the heart would form its own auxiliary blood supply.

The doctor was straightforward in speaking to me, not minimizing the seriousness of his patient's condition but encouraging me. Surgery, he said, still wasn't called for at this time.

"I believe your husband can be monitored with a program of medication, diet, and exercise," Peter Bruno told me. "In the meantime, I'm consulting with a group at Cornell Medical School to examine these films and corroborate my findings."

Bruce left St. John's Hospital a day later, a bit paler following the rigors of his second brush with death, but more determined than ever not to be discouraged. For my part, however, I was a wreck. I had lived so long in blissful ignorance, unaware of the time bomb ticking in my husband's chest. Now, it seemed, the more I knew about my husband's illness, the more cautious and overwrought I became. I had been so optimistic about the results of the angiogram; now I worried over what the next procedure might cause or reveal.

Isn't it true that, so often, it's easier to cope with the unknown than to face up to the known?

Life returned to its revised version of "normal" routine, as the summer came to an end. Dr. Bruno had informed us that cardiologists don't usually see patients unless referred by an internist or general practitioner; so we needed to find a doctor to replace our recently retired family physician. In our rapidly growing suburban community, this news immediately presented a problem. Most of the established, well-regarded local physicians—their medical practices already overloaded—had closed their offices to new patients some time ago. Only the new arrivals, fresh out of medical school and eager for business, were taking on new patients. I wanted Bruce to be under the care of a reputable internist, not someone just starting a practice.

Again I felt a wave of panic. The cardiologist was dismissing his patient, and although Dr. Bruno assured us he would be available to follow Bruce's condition, we knew that he expected us to select a physician to fill the intermediary medical role.

Throughout this period, Bruce continued to have routine stress tests, along with a special program of regular exercise on the treadmill, rowing machine, and stationary bicycle, monitored by the rehabilitation staff associated with the cardiologist's office. I was thankful for this new dimension to his care while we pursued our search for the right internist. Finally, God's providence led us to become patients of Dr. David E. Weeks, chief of internal medicine at the Health Sciences Center and hospital at our nearby State University of New York.

My confidence soared immediately upon meeting Dr. Weeks. His maturity, his experience, his compassion and understanding were evident from the first. But becoming patients of a physician on the staff of University Hospital presented a new wrinkle, for Peter Bruno was not on staff there; he was affiliated with the older local and competing hospitals. The labyrinthine ways of medical politics prevented easy communication between those two doctors.

I believe in God's providence and its direct application to our lives. Even in the choice of doctors, God's provision for us slowly began to reveal itself. To Dr. Weeks, Bruce's coronary symptoms seemed to match the description of a condition called *silent ischemia*. Remarkably, his colleague Dr. Peter F. Cohn is one of the foremost experts in this field. Chief of cardiology at University Hospital, head of that department in the SUNY at Stony Brook medical school, editor of *Cardiology Review*, and author, with his wife, Joan, of *Heart Talk: Preventing and Coping with Silent and Painful Heart Disease*, Dr. Cohn was just the right person to treat my husband.

Silent ischemia, we learned, is a phenomenon in which a heart attack strikes without the typical warning signs of anginal distress. Bruce is one of those 3 or 4 million Americans identified as "asymptomatic cornonary artery disease patients." Believing that such patients are in constant danger of fatal heart attack without help from any of the body's preliminary warning system, Cohn had been testing a program for observing subjects by having them wear a miniature EKG machine, called a Holter monitor, while conducting their lives as normally as possible for forty-eight hours. Each patient keeps an hour-by-hour diary over the two days. By examining the EKG printout and correlating it to the activities recorded in the diary, researchers can determine how often and how many silent ischemia incidents occur and what, if anything, contributes to these dangerous changes in the heart's condition.

We held a final consultation with Dr. Bruno and received his blessing in transferring Bruce's care to physicians at University Hospital.

*   *   *

In March 1986, Dr. Cohn asked Bruce to become one of ten subjects in his ongoing study. This meant having a set of electrodes attached to his chest for forty-eight hours at a time, wearing a device much like a portable radio—*sans* headphones—while going about his daily business. Except for not being able to shower for two days and having some difficulty wearing a business suit, it's no major inconvenience. Bruce has learned how to play golf while wearing the monitor, and we often joke about what its printouts show after he's watched Jane Fonda or some other gorgeous creature on video!

Up to the time of this writing, Bruce has continued to be a test subject for Peter Cohn's periodic studies. He likes knowing that by his participation he may be contributing in a small way toward helping millions of people with heart disease survive and learn to live with their condition.

But even such an advantage as having a world-renowned expert as one's personal cardiologist has a way, over time, of lulling one into a less vigilant, more comfortable style of living. As years passed, the heart attack itself receded like any episode from the past, and we drifted into some of our old ways. In fact, I found "diet" a subject Bruce increasingly refused to discuss. I noticed that, in some respects, he had blocked out much of the heart attack's unpleasantness and simply picked up where he'd left off—except that golf now substituted for running.

Occasionally, he thought about the numbers on the bathroom scale, along with a low-fat, low-cholesterol diet, but I noticed how much more often he was enjoying forbidden foods, especially when eating out at a splendid restaurant. Our homelife, now as just a couple, seemed increasingly more placid. Perhaps aging was the major factor, but I believed that the "Type-A personality" I'd married had somehow mellowed. His old characteristics manifested themselves every so often, but it seemed to me that Bruce was accepting life's imperfections somewhat more graciously. So, I reasoned, why not allow him an occasional treat?

All this, I say, lulled us into complacency.

In the spring of 1988, six years after the heart attack, Dr. Cohn told Bruce to prepare for another angiogram, with the possibility of angioplasty to follow. A relatively new procedure, introduced to the American medical scene in the late 1970s, the technique known medically as "percutaneous transluminal coronary angioplasty" uses a catheter containing a balloon to reach arterial blockage. At the point of blockage, the balloon is inflated and presses the plaque back against the artery wall. This procedure can open narrowed arteries, restoring some of the normal circulation needed for the heart's well-being. Angioplasty isn't foolproof, however; in up to 25 percent of the cases, vessels close down again within months. Up to 10 percent of those who receive angioplasty need bypass surgery within a year.

This news of another angiogram threw me back into a state of emotional frenzy. My apprehensions mirrored the terror of six years earlier. I relived that ordeal down to its every minute. I scheduled an appointment of my own with Dr. Cohn, to discuss my anxiety and to be sure that he was aware of the scare during Bruce's previous angiogram. He reassured me by telling me how the procedure's techniques have improved since 1982, informing me that his team now performs several angiograms each day without difficulty. Furthermore, he suspected that Bruce's heart might have incurred additional blockage since 1982, making such action well-advised.

For his part, Bruce seemed eager for both the angiogram and the possible angioplasty. In April 1988, angiography revealed that Dr. Cohn's suspicions were correct: The left anterior descending artery was now 99 percent blocked, and a second artery had increased in blockage to 90 percent. Angioplasty was recommended for two weeks later. Bruce signed up, as if for a golf outing.

He spent those two weeks preparing me with pep talks and prayer. We had seen television reports about angioplasty and read accounts of its benefits. We knew that it was preferable to bypass surgery. But the doctor scheduled to perform Bruce's angioplasty, Dr. John P. Dervan, looked so young! Hardly as old as our older son! Furthermore, somebody had done him the disservice of describing him to me as "a hotshot." Just what I didn't want for my husband!

But Peter Cohn claimed that John Dervan, director of the Cardiac Catheterization Lab at University Hospital, was among the best in the business. Even though the blockage in one artery was in such a position as to make it difficult to reach, Dr.Cohn assured me that Dr. Dervan could do it, if anyone could.

"Furthermore," he told me, "there's no such thing as an *old* angioplasty specialist. This is a new technique, and it's a young man's field."

Still, I wanted further confirmation; so, without Bruce's knowledge, I went straight to the top. Through one of Bruce's favorite former students, a young Presbyterian pastor named Norman Koop, I contacted his father, then the Surgeon General of the United States, Dr. C. Everett Koop. Busy as he was, Dr. Koop took time to call back, not once but twice; then he wrote to Bruce—again, not once, but twice—following his surgery. The Surgeon General assured me that angioplasty was the next step indicated and that I should feel blessed to be in such competent hands. He promised his own prayers for us.

So we went forward. Dr. Dervan's mastery of his art produced two wider channels, with both arteries showing only 30 percent blockage remaining.

Back home again, Nurse Ratchett took command. This time, the patient was docile and obedient. The rules were simple.

"Angioplasty isn't a cure," Dr. Cohn had told Bruce. "It's a procedure that pushes back the clock."

For a while, depending on the individual patient's propensity for producing arterial plaque and regimen for fighting it, the arteries can remain largely unblocked. Certainly, if you don't put excess fat into your system, your arteries have a better chance of remaining open. But we understood that angioplasty is no guarantee that further treatment—including bypass surgery—won't be needed.

Once again, we found ourselves at a new threshold. Knowing that Bruce now enjoyed less restricted arteries made us feel that he had been reborn. Modern technology's new discoveries in the field of medicine had given him the possibility of a third chance at a productive life. We covenanted together and with God not to waste that chance.

At this writing, it's been eighteen months since the successful angioplasty. Bruce continues to do well. With the help of Dr. Joan Cohn's delicious recipes in *Heart Talk*, with the surge of information concerning oat bran, with a regular program of exercise, and with my husband's co-operation, we eat well and eat healthy.

Yet, I'm more keenly aware than ever before that each day is a gift. Family and friends often ask me about Bruce, "How is he doing?" In the beginning of this story, I would have answered defensively, "Fine, I trust," immediately feeling a jolt of uneasiness.

Don't they think he looks well? Do they think he's doing too much? Does everyone think I'm responsible for his well-being?

Over these several years, I have come slowly to the realization that my husband's health is, first, in the hands of God, then primarily the result of choices Bruce makes regarding his own life. I'm there to support, encourage, provide a proper diet, and—yes—challenge him to keep up the daily regimen prescribed by his physicians.

But I no longer feel totally responsible for his health.

He's the type of man who will never sit back and feel that there's nothing to do. He is a creative person, never happier than when he has a publisher's deadline to meet or a business trip to prepare for. A vacation to him is always the same: a few days of leisure, then he's restless to resume his normal activities. For instance, to Bruce more than twenty minutes at the beach would seem just unbearable!

I have also learned that he believes that the quality of his life is more important than its length. If he can be productive, he feels fulfilled. Accepting this, our life together is reasonably balanced, happy, and hopeful.

Illness in itself is often a blessing in disguise. It has a way of letting us know that we aren't in control. Illness forces us to face the truth about ourselves, bringing out characteristics that are sometimes admirable, sometimes shameful. Illness robs us of our independence, but illness also compels our utter dependence upon God's mercy.

Illness makes us grow up quickly. When either one of us is sick, we can't indulge ourselves in selfishness, if that marriage is to survive. Our character is sorely tested, as is the very marriage bond itself. It will either erode with the stress or be cemented so that its foundation becomes even stronger.

In many ways, these years since 1982 have been better than our first twenty-five years together. We've each had to ask ourselves, *What is the most important part of my relationship?* As I think of my marriage, I'm honestly able to say today—as perhaps I couldn't have said before 1982—my husband is my lover, my reason for being who I am.

The future is unknown. In God's plan, we gratefully accept each new and healthy day as a gift. Is every day perfect? Of course, I wish I could answer yes, but that would be untrue. Life isn't designed to be easy or perfect. We are constantly being tested and more often than not, I have to acknowledge that I'm not in control. That's still difficult for me, but I'm trying.

Perhaps because I'm an elementary school teacher, my mind makes an anagram out of the ABCs. The words *accept, believe,* and *commit* have a message for me. If I'm learning through life's experiences, I must first learn to accept God's divine will for my life. This means that I will not always be happy with what comes my way; but I must learn to trust that God's purpose is greater than my own desire. Next, believing that God has a plan for me and that He knows what's best, I must learn to trust Him and not rely on my own willfulness. Finally, I need to learn to commit myself wholeheartedly to each new day, maintaining a serenity and, above all, a sense of humor.

The more I become aware of these ABCs—*accept, believe,*

commit—the better I seem to be able to cope with situations that are out of my power to control.

When Bruce invited me to join him in writing this book, the prospect of producing my part—these five chapters—initially frightened me. Since graduate school, I have written nothing but lesson plans and thank-you notes. Once I agreed, however, I was determined that every word attributed to me would be my own. But it wasn't just the daunting task of helping to write a book that scared me. I knew it wouldn't be easy to deal with my emotions all over again, especially those I have suppressed for years.

Yet talking with you, our reader, has been a growing experience for me, requiring me to look face-to-face at who I am at this moment. As this chapter and my part in the writing of this book ends, I would like to feel that, in a very real way, I have reached a new beginning, thankful for the challenges of yesterday and looking ahead with renewed courage and faith to tomorrow's opportunities.

12
A Change of Heart

Would you believe I almost blew my second chance at life?

Lory has told you about how our lives were changed by the effects of my—perhaps, more accurately, *our*—heart attack. She has also taken much of the blame for my falling back into old, careless habits, eventually reflected in a cholesterol count that soared again to dangerous heights. I guess it's time for true confessions.

Released from the hospital in late June of 1982, with words of cheer and admonition from my doctor and nurses, with a long-suffering and earnest wife committed to my welfare—and, may I add, with all the high aspirations I could muster—it wasn't long before I slipped back into my old ways.

You might not expect that someone whose life had been spared would ever again indulge in practices that, for him, are so potentially lethal. For many of us mortals, however, establishing and holding fast to a healthy diet requires an extra measure of grace.

Perhaps you're not addicted to Heavenly Hash ice cream! Count your blessings! I had a special weakness for ice cream or any other whole milk product. I never liked skim milk, so I insisted on stocking up on half gallons of fully loaded homogenized milk, along with Half-and-Half for our unleaded coffee, and, occasionally, whipped cream on desserts. I preferred real butter to margarine, and I spread it liberally on everything that seemed to ask for it, including croissants and pecan ring.

I'd order bacon and eggs for breakfast, steak and fries or calves' liver and onions for dinner. I regularly turned my nose up at chicken, turkey (except at Thanksgiving), and fish. But cheese was my real craving—cheese and crackers, cheese toppings on my baked potatoes, macaroni and cheese, cheeseburgers with double cheese, vegetables au gratin—*anything* with cheese.

So, in spite of Lory's best intentions to provide healthy meals, I thwarted her whenever my appetite demanded, and she succumbed to my insistence. After all, whose life was it anyway?

You don't need a complete summary of everything else that happened. You have learned enough about me already to understand how, little by little, Bruce Lockerbie returned to his Type-A habits. But, as you may have guessed, my relapse into careless living also involved running. Well, actually, trying to substitute fast walking for running.

Dr. Bruno had declined to give me permission to run. "I can't stop you, of course," he told me at my first appointment after leaving the hospital, "but I won't go on record as recommending running either. There's still too much irregularity we call arrhythmia. You'll have to content yourself with walking, at least for now."

I listened, but I didn't hear what he said. I was determined to return to running. My determination resulted from just plain-and-nasty pride. I had built up such an appalling contempt for lethargic and unathletic men who followed the fad into jogging, I vowed never to become one of them. "A runner till I die" was my motto.

I never quite achieved that dream, partly because I finally conceded that, if I couldn't run as fast as my contemporary competitors, I preferred not to run at all. Okay, take running from me, and I'll replace it with fast walking or striding. I had already made lame attempts, you may recall, in the corridors of the hospital, until the doctor slowed me down and ordered me to remove my stopwatch. But once at home, I reverted to my competitive nature.

I had been instructed to take up to three short walks each day. A circuit was marked around our house and through neighboring woods—about one-eighth of a mile, half a lap around a track. Early on, Lory accompanied me on each stroll. I needed her beside me because, for the first two days at home, I quivered like a newborn colt with every unsteady step. It was astonishing how atrophied my legs seemed.

But by the end of my first week home, I was deliberately looking for occasions to walk that would be inconvenient for Lory, just so I could walk faster than she allowed. I invented a pattern of walking that included at least one rapid-paced loop on the watch. Barely back to life, I was already doing time trials!

My next move took me from the path around our house

to the half-mile trail encircling Stony Brook School's play-ing fields; in time, to the roads I used to enjoy running. At home, I logged each day's performance, as faithfully as when I kept a training diary before a major race.

Faster! Faster! And the point is, there was no point!

During that same summer of 1982, someone asked if I had ever considered golf as a form of exercise. I had played a few rounds as a teenager, a very few more as a younger man, enough to discover that my regressive left-handedness asserted itself when I stood over a golf ball. Apart from an amusement park's miniature golf putter, Lory had never touched a club.

For my forty-seventh birthday, the family gave me a set of Jack Nicklaus signature woods and irons; soon after, we outfitted Lory. In September, we began playing nine holes after school on an executive course, each of us pulling a handcart. Walking the golf course was much slower than my timed treks on the roads, but I noticed how much more weary I felt after only ninety minutes of par-3 golf than after an hour's brisk walk. Not until I met Dr. Peter F. Cohn did I understand what might be the reason for the difference.

Golf took hold of me with the same passion I had known, once upon a time, competing in track. I became an addict, playing whenever possible on one of Long Island's overcrowded public courses; a weekend fan of the tele-vised tournaments, a subscriber to golfing publications, a viewer of home instructional videos, a frequenter of golf shops where I browsed in search of the next set of clubs that would ensure lower scores. Eventually, I joined the Nissequogue Golf Club, a magnificent course overlooking Long Island Sound, just so I could play whenever I wished.

In almost no time, I recreated the same conditions of stress that had been part of my running. Just as I knew where, in a given race, to apply the aerobic pressure that would overcome my oxygen debt, so on a given golf course, I began to think about what shot was needed here to compensate for the lie of my ball or the dangers of the sand traps ahead or how to make up for the poor shot I'd just shanked. Just as during the earlier part of the day, I used to daydream about my afternoon workout, so now I found myself contemplating the next round of golf and how I could improve its outcome.

I took up playing with other friends; soon I was competing *against* them. I couldn't be content with what every real golfer knows: that you play, first, against the course and, next, against yourself. I was too intent on beating the other guy's score! Few of them were real golfers; mostly just beginning hackers, like me, and it grated on me whenever one of them could score better than my as yet undeveloped skills allowed.

By spring 1983, I felt ready to seek out new challenges, so Lory and I went to Pinehurst, North Carolina, one of the shrines of golf, on a three-day package. As we drove our cart toward the first tee, I could feel my pulse racing.

"My palms are sweaty," my terrified bride wailed. "Just like, when I was kid, before a piano recital!"

Such tension! Such frustration! In the presence of awesome natural and man-made beauty, such ugliness of temperament and temper!

At the end of the first day's eighteen holes, we mounted the steps to the broad porch of the Pinehurst Hotel, fell each into a wicker rocking chair, and slept with exhaustion. We dragged ourselves out to the course for the second day's round, following which we almost slept through the dinner hour. Thank God, a heavy rain kept us from playing at all on the third day; otherwise, we'd have killed ourselves.

Why was golf so much more strenuous than a hard run had ever been?

Work also took its toll. Administrative and teaching duties piled upon books to be completed and another season of high-intensity college and seminary lectures. Looking over old diaries, I see that, in September alone, I spent half the month away from home, nine more days in October, a dozen more in November before Thanksgiving. For me, nothing had changed, except I was now checking all luggage curbside at the airport, instead of carrying steamer trunks on board my flights.

Several events helped to slow me down. In February 1983, Lory had been booked to accompany me on a trip to the West Coast. We planned to fly to Los Angeles, drive to Santa Barbara, and stay for a week in a favorite hotel, from which I would commute for my speaking appointments. Sunny Southern California would be our midwinter respite.

As we left Stony Brook and drove toward Kennedy Airport on a Friday afternoon, the first flake of snow caressed our windshield. By the time we arrived at American Airlines' terminal, a blizzard had descended, officially closing JFK Airport. Leaving to return home was out of the question; several people who tried were found dead in their cars when the storm finally ended. We were stuck for fifty-two hours, sleeping Friday night on our suitcases, Saturday night on the carpeted floor in the Admirals Club lounge, courtesy of a Stony Brook alumnus also stranded in the terminal. We finally boarded a plane at ten o'clock Sunday evening, bound not for Los Angeles but Portland,

Oregon, via Salt Lake City. By that time, we were willing to go anywhere!

We checked into our Santa Barbara sunshine spa several days late and somewhat bruised from our misadventure. I had missed my first lecture engagement. Yet, remarkably, that inconvenience became an experience of grace. The Bible tells of God's common grace that provides seedtime and harvest for the just and the unjust alike, but we recognized several other manifestations of common grace during our enforced weekend at the airport: courtesy among strangers in observing other people's rights to space and privacy; good humor under shared unpleasant conditions; at all times, exceptional service by American Airlines' employees marooned with us and still willing to offer what help they could; most important, perhaps, in such trying circumstances, God's common grace in restraining evil from perpetrating its worst among us.

But one thing more: Being snowed in at Kennedy Airport taught me who's really in charge of my timetable. Not the Federal Aviation Administration nor the airline computer nor my flight's captain; not the air traffic controllers nor the friendly weatherman on TV; certainly not me. For years I prided myself on never missing a booking. Late, maybe; absent, never. You know: "Neither snow, nor rain, nor heat, nor gloom of night stays these couriers. . . ." To keep that record, I would go to extraordinary means, if necessary. On occasion, eager to make a connecting flight, I'd jostle other passengers to push my way down the aisle of a plane, rushing to make my appointment to speak on Christian love!

As the hours of our snowbound delay inched by, I leafed through my New Testament, reading hit-and-miss, until I came to Luke's Gospel. In the first chapter, my eyes fell on the familiar story of Gabriel's visitation to Mary. I read again of the young girl in Nazareth, confronted by a fearful summons, who yet learned to say, "Be it unto me according to thy will." In her initial shock and dismay, I caught a glimpse of my own caricature, and I laughed. I knew how far short of living in submission to God's will my frenetic tendencies had often carried me.

If ever one could claim an odd site for a vision of transcendent reality, sitting on a suitcase in a snowbound airport qualifies. That afternoon, I jotted down the following words, a modern version of Mary's song of praise and submission.

> What more can I say?
> What more can I demand?
> I never meant to question or presume.
> The will and work of God are His to know,
> Mine to obey.
> My times are in His hand,
> My threads of life are stretched upon His
> loom;
> He weaves the pattern, and it must be so.
> Submission to His will in full accord:
> I am the humble servant of the Lord.
>
> What more can I say?
> What more can I require?
> Who will believe what God has done for me?
> I only ask that God, who knows my heart,
> Prepare the way,
> So that the trust love can inspire
> May overrule all doubt and help us see
> The miracle in which we play a part.

Submission to His will in full accord:
We are the willing servants of the Lord.

Lory has told you already how, in the spring of 1986, I came under the care of Dr. Peter F. Cohn who, with his wife, taught me some graphic lessons about myself. I was participating in his silent heart disease study, repeatedly wearing the Holter monitor device for forty-eight-hour periods. Never during those times, nor at any other, did I feel the chest pains commonly associated with angina; I was wholly asymptomatic. Yet, as the doctor later informed me, in every forty-eight-hour span, the ten members of our study group were recording as many as seventeen episodes of life-threatening damage to the heart, caused by insufficient blood flow. Some of these episodes were brief, others lasted up to thirty minutes.

What brought about these changes? Physical exertion could certainly be blamed, but few of us were digging ditches or carrying hods of bricks. In my case, I do most of my work sitting at a word processor or talking on the telephone. Little energy expended there.

Then Peter Cohn proceeded to conduct a demonstration for his medical students, using me as his subject. Asked to lie down on an examining table and hooked up to an EKG machine, my initial pulse rate was a calm fifty-eight to sixty beats per minute. Then, as I recall, the overhead lights in the room were turned on brighter, the group of observers came closer around the table, and Dr. Cohn bent over my face, asking me to solve arithmetic problems, mostly in subtraction. He began with a number, then said, "Add seven. Take away nine. Take away nine. Take away nine. Add seven." His instructions grew more and more tormenting in tone. "Faster, faster," he demanded. I could feel the dampness of my armpits, the dryness of my throat, as I clutched for the right answers to his persistent, staccato barrage of numbers. It was worse than any fifth-grade recitation of the multiplication tables.

His experiment lasted only a few minutes, by which time my pulse rate had accelerated to more than ninety beats per minute—as much as if I'd been working out on a rowing machine or stationary bicycle. Released from the table, I sat up almost groggy from my sudden and surprising weakness.

I had experienced *stress*—a required, public exhibition of my arithmetical skills before an audience of strangers; a mental effort to please, to avoid embarrassment, to prove something to somebody. The whole experience had been free from any physical transfer of energy we might recognize as work; yet its effect was as wearying as, perhaps, running up three flights of stairs.

Why, on any given day, had I ended a difficult telephone conversation or a taxing lecture or the struggle to get the text of a particular paragraph just so—routine activities in my normal day—wondering why I felt so tired? Why had my father, after a strenuous Sunday morning service, gone home to our parsonage, needing to sleep during the afternoon to be ready for another sermon delivery that evening? Why had I often ended a round of golf, far more weary from the stress of stroking the ball successfully than from the walking itself? Now I knew. *Stress*.

Later, I learned of similar experiments to induce stress and its related effects among silent heart disease patients at Boston's Brigham and Women's Hospital, including reading aloud, even giving a five-minute speech on one's own personal faults. Each simulation of a stress-related experience seemed linked to restricted blood flow and risk of further heart damage.

What this meant for me was this: The fact that I was carrying on my life and work without chest pain, with no numbness in my arms, no shortness of breath, was itself a delusion. My claim that I felt perfectly well had almost nothing to do with my true state of health. I was, I always would be, a person whose heart had been damaged and needed help to perform its work. That help could take any of several forms: total replacement by a heart transplanted from somebody else's body, repair by surgery, or assistance by medication for increased blood supply.

At this point, the cardiologist introduced his wife, Dr. Joan K. Cohn, a psychotherapist also on the faculty of the State University of New York at Stony Brook. Until this conversation with Dr. Joan Cohn, I hadn't really faced up to what it means to live as fully as possible following a heart attack. From her, as from no one else to date, I learned the value of affirming my state-of-being, without whining or attaching self-pity to that description. What did it mean to be recovering from a heart attack? It certainly couldn't mean—in my case—sitting idle in momentary anticipation of the end. Nor could it mean living a truncated existence, hoping that this flight of stairs or that icy blast of wind wouldn't be the final straw too great for my heart to bear. For me, it must mean a sensible program of medical care, prescription drugs, exercise, diet, and faith, combined with a happy marriage and rewarding work.

When I told her, for instance, about my pleasure in eating heaping scoops of rich ice cream, Joan Cohn smiled and said, "Think of it as poison."

That'll be the day, I thought to myself.

174

A few days later, on a grocery shopping trip, I stood behind a grossly overweight woman whose two shopping carts were overflowing with every possible item of junk food on the supermarket's shelves: gallons of ice cream, oversized packages of chips, huge containers of artificial whipped cream, cream-filled cakes and other pastries.

As I looked at these cholesterol high explosives, I thought of Dr. Joan Cohn's advice, *Think of it as poison.* I looked again, and sure enough, there was a skull-and-crossbones on every package.

Both David Weeks and Peter Cohn assured me that angioplasty was a prudent next step in my cardiac maintenance. On May 4, 1988, Dr. John P. Dervan attempted to open two coronary arteries, both blocked almost solid with fatty substance. For the more difficult blockage in the left anterior descending or LAD artery, Dervan had obtained special permission to employ a new catheter still in experimental use at that time.

During angioplasty, the patient lies under X-ray cameras centered above the chest. To his right, behind a large window, stand a group of observing physicians and students; among them, prepped for business, are the anesthesiologist and cardiac surgeon who will perform any emergency operation required. To the patient's left, a large clock records the unrelated passage of time. A television monitor plays the scene going on within, as the doctor inserts the catheter through a vessel in the groin, then feeds it up and through the body toward the heart. A radioactive dye helps identify the instrument's path. When the tip of the catheter reaches the point of blockage, a balloon on the end of the catheter is inflated. Then, like a battering ram, it charges the barricade of plaque, shoving the debris aside, pressing it back against the blood vessel's wall.

Meanwhile, the patient is fully alert and participating in the procedure, breathing on command, holding that breath against his seemingly desperate need to gasp for more: "Hold it, hold it, hold it, hold it!" Feeling a burning sensation reminiscent of the only warning signs he ever knew; sensing a fleeting instant in which the weight of the whole world—well, at least a very heavy sandbag—has been lowered onto his chest. Then blessed relief as the surgeon orders, "You can breathe normally now."

After seventy-five minutes by the clock on the wall, the doctor comes around the surgical table to his patient's head.

"I've been able to reach that awkward location in the LAD," he reports. "In fact, I've been there for the last fifteen minutes. Things are going well."

The patient can see, even through the surgical mask, that the young doctor is smiling. The patient too is smiling, rejoicing, praising God.

The procedure continues to go so well that from others at the opposite end of the table—as well as in the observation room—the patient can hear exclamations of congratulations and delight.

"Excellent!"

"Super!"

"Terrific!"

Three hours later, following close observation in a recovery room and transfer to CCU, the patient learns that both blocked arteries have been opened so that only thirty percent blockage remains. The news is rapturously satisfying to all.

Three weeks later, following a letter of thanks, a reply

comes from Surgeon General Koop, revealing once more his warmth and compassion:

> Thanks for keeping me informed about your progress. So few people do. And that deprives me of what must be a number of episodes of Thanksgiving. Delighted things went so well and that I could at least have an opinion. The procedure you had is really quite remarkable and it might last you forever.

Two months after the angioplasty, Dr. Cohn asked if Lory and I would care to be included in a film being made for showing in hospitals to encourage recent heart attack survivors. The broadcaster Larry King would host the film, to be called "A Change of Heart." We agreed.

Director Dennis Knife and his crew came to our home and spent an entire July day filming our part of the interviews. Once more Lory and I relived our experience together, this time hopeful that our story and its visual representation of our joy in reclaiming every good and perfect gift from our gracious God would inspire someone else to go on from his or her hospital room to an even more productive and healthier life. I was filmed walking along our Stony Brook harborfront, hitting my 5-iron a ton, eating an oat bran muffin, taking a daily aspirin along with my prescribed medication.

Interviewing the other families and editing the film for final production took several months. In mid-January 1989, we received our copy of the videotape. Larry King made an effective, if sometimes earthy, narrator, communicating with his audience from personal experience based on his own near-fatal heart attack. I watched and listened to the tape like someone in a hospital a thousand miles away. I heard the self-revelations and platitudes, the well-intentioned advice, from several recovered heart attack survivors; and, from one long-suffering wife, a commentary on how her husband's heart attack had affected their marriage.

Naturally, I was most taken by the story of someone named Bruce Lockerbie, speaking, as it were, just to me about his emotional reaction to his heart attack, his struggle to recover and learn from that illness, his certainty that faith had sustained him. I heard and saw a lovely woman named Lory recount how, at last, her husband had become a much more placid and contented person.

I decided, then and there, I wanted to be that man.

13
Taking the Sting Out of Death

Our friend Marvin Goldberg was the first person to alert us to the implausible news: Pan Am Flight #103 had exploded over Scotland, its wreckage falling upon a quiet country town called Lockerbie.

Until December 21, 1988, our family name had seemed strange to most ears. But since the terrorist tragedy, with the loss of some 270 lives in the air and on the ground, the name Lockerbie carries with it less unfamiliarity but more sorrow. Remarkably often, when someone recognizes the name and makes the connection—on a supermarket checkout line, at a hotel registration desk, during introductions at the golf club—the questions that follow reveal empathy and common grieving: "Is your family from that town? Did you lose anyone in the disaster?"

Strictly speaking, the answers are no. Like any tourists abroad, our immediate family has visited the ancestral village, but we're not from that town; we didn't lose anyone we knew in that firestorm. At least, that's how we responded initially.

But more and more, we've come to think of Lockerbie, Scotland, and the calamity there as a symbol of our time.

Death in modern society is both so impersonal and so intimate. Technology can be programmed to kill at distances of hundreds of miles; technology can also zero in on an individual mother's anguish and collapse as she learns of her baby's random and heartless slaughter. So, viewing the aftermath of the Pan Am #103 event, we've learned again two lessons about death: its irrationality and its commonality.

Just as there is no reasonable way to explain why a bombed plane's flaming debris should have rained destruction upon a single town's populace, so death never makes sense because death is born out of chaos and confusion. Death disrupts, death destroys, and laughs at any cry for explanations.

Yet, in spite of death's irrationality, a sense of community exists among those who survive. John Donne, the seventeen-century poet and dean of St. Paul's Cathedral, wrote,

> No man is an island, entire of itself; every man is a
> piece of the continent, a part of the main. . . . Any
> man's death diminishes me, because I am involved in
> mankind; and therefore never send to know for
> whom the bell tolls; it tolls for thee.

Death creates a bond among its survivors, so that—in a manner of speaking—all of us who are "involved in mankind" dwell together in that same rural village, our lives under a curse, yet looking for mutual encouragement to believe in our eventual deliverance from being held hostage to terror.

Since we began writing this book, a colleague's infant daughter and several former students at Stony Brook have died. During a recent springtime, three parents of current students died only days apart of each other. Within our family, our daughter-in-law Belinda's mother, Sarah Polk, has died of ALS, Lou Gehrig's disease; and Bruce's stepfather, George Johnston, has died of complications following surgery.

"In the midst of life we are in death. . . ."

But we don't talk much about it. Only when death seems to mean release from suffering can we bring ourselves to wish it soon, speaking of—even hoping for—death's untimely arrival as a blessing, a divine deliverance.

Even as professed Christian believers, we don't commonly like to talk about death, least of all our own. Why? Because death remains, as Job termed it, "the king of terrors." Yet isn't death supposed to be different somehow for those who celebrate the Easter miracle and sing, "O Death, where is thy sting? O grave, where is thy victory?"

Death's mystery is especially perplexing to believing Christians. On the one hand, we worship the God to whom we ascribe omnipotence as Creator and Sustainer of life; at the same time, we accept as God's permissive will the fact that

> To every thing there is a season, and a time to every
> purpose under the heaven: A time to be born, and a
> time to die. . . .

We treasure life as a precious gift from God; so it is. Some of us stand in our churches, Sunday by Sunday, and recite,

> I believe in . . . the resurrection of the body, and the life everlasting;

yet we walk out the door, still frozen by death's chilling stare. Some quote Bible promises, making it clear that "to be with Christ . . . is far better." Others sing exuberant songs of faith, assuring themselves and us that,

> *In the sweet by and by,*
> *We shall meet on that beautiful shore.*

Yet many of us cry at funerals. Why? For whom?

In his titanic struggle against God, Satan's last weapon is death, and only death can defeat death. That's the reason for the Incarnation, for Christmas: As spirit, God can't die; so the Incarnate Christ accepts the role, taking the full measure of all that death can deal—the humiliation of human hatred, its physical pain, the awful anguish of betrayal—including the sin with which Satan burdens the whole human race. As the Letter to the Hebrews makes plain,

> Forasmuch then as the children are partakers of flesh and blood, he also himself likewise took part of the same; that *through death he might destroy him that had the power of death,* that is, the devil.
>
> Hebrews 2:14; italics mine

182

To the very end, Satan attempts to deflect Jesus Christ from His purpose—the Gethsemane plea to have the cup removed, the cry of abandonment from the cross, the ultimate temptation to remove himself from the cross and compel belief through spectacle; yet the Lord Jesus Christ bears the full weight of death by crucifixion.

And He wins the victory! He descends to the grave, the Stricken Hero; He rises from the grave, the Conquering Hero. But this victory is more than an epic encounter between Good and Evil; it has both personal and universal consequences. It affects—or can affect—every one of us today because, as the Letter to the Hebrews further states, along with destroying Satan's power of death, Jesus Christ's victory can also

> deliver them who *through fear of death* were all their
> lifetime subject to bondage.
> Hebrews 2:15; italics mine

Here, then, for every Christian to affirm, is the truth about death. In human terms, death remains fearsome. Like a wounded beast, Satan remains a threatening foe until that day when his power is finally taken from him. But until then, thanks be to God, Jesus Christ has won for us the right to be delivered from that slavery to fear. For, again, as John Donne wrote,

> *One short sleep past, we wake eternally,*
> *And Death shall be no more: Death, thou shalt die!*

But please, don't mistake this Christian view of death we espouse as being, in any way, the same as sheer fatalism. A belief in the whims of fate is no better than a superstitious fear of Friday the thirteenth or of walking under a ladder. To live under the control of fate means living as a victim of some impersonal, indifferent force. No matter what one does, fate or The Fates will decide your doom.

But Christians don't need to live like losers in some vast cosmic dice game. Christians are never victims; in fact, Christians need never be either pessimistic or optimistic, as though somehow their ultimate destiny were still in doubt. For a Christian, the truly biblical virtue is *hopefulness* because our hope is secure in the promises of Jesus Christ, who has set us free from the fear of death.

When we board an airplane, we pray for God's protection in travel and for the wisdom of the pilot and crew. Then we buckle up, obeying federal law, and follow the flight attendants' instructions. If we were mere fatalists, we'd trust ourselves to luck or chance or fate, believing that such powers have already picked the date and that nothing can alter their indifferent will.

Christians believe otherwise. We have an obligation to the God who gave us life to conserve and preserve it responsibly. By our careful diet, by our habits of work and play, by our necessary sleep, by prudent medical maintenance, and by sensible choices, we live to God's glory for as long as that life can mirror its Maker.

But how can we ever be ready for death—our own or someone else's? Death is never convenient, never easy. Worst of all, death is never wholly painless. A toddler stumbles into an uncovered well; a casual passerby is struck by a ricocheting bullet from a drug dealer's weapon; a brilliant scholar is crushed by a falling tree; a promising young leader—an athlete, a gifted communicator with his peers—is cut down by heart disease; a young wife and mother, in seemingly perfect health, collapses and dies from a cerebral hemorrhage; a bus full of church youths is rammed by a drunken driver, exploding and incinerating its occupants; a terrorist bomb brings down a plane—and the world mourns.

Why do we cry at funerals? Because, even as we may rejoice that the angels and saints are greeting our loved one, that Christ our Brother is welcoming him or her home, we feel the pain of parting. We cry, just as Jesus Himself wept at the grave of His friend Lazarus. We cry for ourselves, perhaps for others who may be grieving even more deeply than we know because they have no faith in a heavenly reunion.

We cry because it is right to cry, that even in Satan's final writhings before he is finally put down, one more of God's creatures must be taken from us—no matter how temporarily. But we also cry in anticipation of that glorious day, when God himself

> shall wipe away all tears from their eyes; and there shall be no more death, neither sorrow, nor crying, neither shall there be any more pain: for the former things are passed away.
>
> Revelation 21:4

Who wouldn't want to have a tear—one trembling tear— to fall when God Himself will wipe them all away?

Death is fearful; death causes pain. To deny any of this is worse than romanticism; it's downright dishonesty. Yet our mourning, proper though it may be, must also be different from the grief of unbelievers in the mercy of God or disbelievers in the power of the Resurrection. Different because, as Saint Paul tells the Thessalonians, we are to "sorrow not, even as others which have no hope." Our bereavement is to be, somehow, distinctive from a pagan's irretrievable loss.

How can we hope to live out our faith, even in the hour of trial? Certainly we may take solace from the Word of God, from our own prayers, and from the prayers of others. We may also find "grace to help in time of need" from various other sources, including grief itself.

We need to accept, as evidence of God's grace, the gift of mourning. Too often, in times of stress, evangelical Christians rush forward to claim their biblical promises without being willing to endure with patience the anguish through which those promises shine. An array of sanctimonious axioms and catchphrases results, reducing genuine *experience* to a pious *effect*, consisting of approved clichés. Then genuine bitterness and anger against God come later, after the superficial *effect* has passed.

We are all fragile believers, more susceptible to the sorrows of death than, in our most lofty moments, we like to admit. So, perhaps, it is best not to attempt to profess how much we believe; it's better to rely on our deeper faith, which has no other way of expressing itself than by "groanings that cannot be uttered."

Nor should many of us dare to presume to be the model Christian, as did Joseph Addison, in a 1719 deathbed letter to his stepson:

> I have sent for you that you may see how a Christian
> can die.

No one can be so sure that we can afford to predict how we'll control our emotions and submit our grief to God's will. What matters is the degree to which we acknowledge, with Saint Paul, that

> none of us liveth to himself, and no man dieth to himself. For whether we live, we live unto the Lord; and whether we die, we die unto the Lord: whether we live, therefore, or die, we are the Lord's.
>
> Romans 14:7, 8

Saint Paul ends his admonition to the Thessalonians, about how to accept the death of a fellow believer, by telling them to comfort or encourage each other with his words of inspired truth. The word *encourage* literally means to strengthen the heart, to hearten oneself or another, to *take heart*.

So we pray for grace, in all the afflictions of life, to take heart by believing God's promises and living by them, in sure and certain hope of the resurrection to eternal life. Then with all the saints, we too may sing,

Free at last! Free at last!
Thank God Almighty, I'm free at last!